# GREAT MOMENTS

# IN SOUTHERN CALIFORNIA SPORTS

RIGHT: On the day before Thanksgiving, 1986, Eric Dickerson was looking airborne for the Rams.

WITH PHOTOGRAPHS BY STAFF PHOTOGRAPHERS
OF THE *LOS ANGELES TIMES* AND OTHERS

# GREAT MOMENTS IN SOUTHERN CALIFORNIA SPORTS

## EARL GUSTKEY

**HARRY N. ABRAMS, INC.,
PUBLISHERS, NEW YORK**

*This is for my wife, Nancy, whose help and encouragement
made this book a thoroughly enjoyable experience.*

For Harry N. Abrams, Inc.:
Editor: Robert Morton
Designer: Rogers Seidman Design

For *Los Angeles Times:*
Project Director: Angela Rinaldi
Photo Research: Gay Raskiewicz

FIRST PAGE: Greg Louganis goes gold again at the Seoul Olympics in 1988 in the springboard competition, four years
after winning in Los Angeles and only a day after cracking his skull on the board in a qualifying dive.

SECOND PAGE: Magic Johnson had Bill Laimbeer and Joe Dumars baffled under the basket in the 1988 NBA finals.

THIRD PAGE: Orel Hershiser gets a well-deserved hug from his battery mate as the 1988 Dodgers win the Series over Oakland.

TITLE PAGES: Carl Lewis wins the 100 meter dash at the 1984 summer games in the Coliseum.

## PICTURE CREDITS

# CONTENTS

# 1800 TO 1899

A trio of *vaqueros* prepare to bring in a grizzly bear for a bull-bear fight.

W hat's the biggest sports event in Southern California?¶ A Rose Bowl game? A Dodger Stadium World Series? A Coliseum Super Bowl? USC vs. UCLA?¶ Pick any one, and you're sure to collect a lot of votes. But that's today. What about, say, 1825? Or 1850? Slip into a time capsule, zip back to the mid-nineteenth century, ask the same question on any dusty street in the Alta California pueblos of Santa Barbara, Los Angeles, or San Diego, and you'd get only one answer.¶ Bull-and-bear fights.¶ A museum in California's Gold Rush country has an old, faded, torn poster, printed in 1850, that reads:¶ "WAR! The celebrated bull-killing bear, General Scott, will fight a bull Sunday the 15th at 2 P.M. at Moquelumne Hill. The bear will be chained by a 20-foot chain in the middle of the arena. The bull will be

perfectly wild, young, of the Spanish breed, and its horns will be of their natural length and will not be sawed off!"

Think the young college and professional sports superstars of Southern California are big today? Chances are, they were no bigger than Ramon Ortega of Ventura County, an 1850s grizzly roper nonpareil. While astride a horse, Ortega could rope a grizzly by a paw and tether it to a tree. Alone.

In pre-Gold Rush California, the region was abundant in grizzly bears. *Ursus horribilis Californicus.* They were lowlands bears, up to eight feet long and weighing up to 1,200 pounds. They were found most commonly in the oaklands of foothills and valleys, and also on the beaches of California. Seventeenth-century mariners mapping the California coast wrote of seeing grizzlies feeding on the carcasses of beached whales and sea lions.

And so when Spanish ranchers began running vast, unfenced cattle operations in California, inevitable man-bear conflicts occurred. And so too did bull-and-bear fights. In old Spain, animal bouts such as lion vs. tiger were not uncommon. The killing of bulls and other animals became a fixture at Spanish fiestas in the fourteenth century.

In every community in Southern California, including the missions at San Diego, San Luis Rey, San Juan Capistrano, San Gabriel, and Santa Barbara, citizens avidly anticipated, watched, and wagered on bull-and-bear fights.

Reading witnesses' accounts of how grizzlies were captured alive in Southern California leads one today to the conclusion that the old vaqueros of the Spanish and Mexican periods might have been the most skilled horsemen who ever lived.

Let's put it this way; if Willie Shoemaker was such a good horseman, could he have

James Walker's painting *Roping the Bear,* made in about 1870, reflects California's Spanish and Mexican periods, when horsemanship was the most admired skill on vast cattle ranchos. The supreme test of rider and horse was the live capture of a grizzly bear, which was then hauled off to a fight to the death with a prime bull. After the Gold Rush, and as California's human population grew, the big ranchos were broken up and the great bears were forced from their habitats in coastal plains and valleys into the mountains. There, they were killed in great numbers by gold miners. By the 1920s the California grizzly was extinct.

roped a grizzly, controlled bear and horse, and tethered the bruin to a tree—unaided?

California historians say bull-and-bear fights were held for three reasons:

—To rid the countryside of the feared grizzlies, which threatened livestock and made travel dangerous. Often, they were shot on sight.

—To showcase the vaqueros' riding and roping skills, which were considerable and were greatly admired in old California society.

—To help celebrate a special occasion at the missions, such as a saint's birthday.

Harold McCracken, in his 1957 book, *The Beast That Walks Like Man,* wrote of the horsemanship required in capturing grizzlies alive: "It was considered the ultimate in thrills and skills. Horsemanship and the use of a lasso were accomplishments of great pride to the vaqueros of old California. Roping grizzlies for a fiesta bull-and-bear fight became their sport of sports."

In an 1873 book, *California: For Health, Pleasure, and Residence,* eastern writer Charles Nordhoff wrote of the vaqueros' horsemanship, after watching a rodeo: "There were some really magnificent feats of horsemanship...and no bull was so wild that he did not find his master. [I observed] feats with the lasso, which are really like jugglery or witchcraft. I have a hundred times watched the fling of the riata, and yet have never in a single instance been able to detect the precise moment of the capture."

The capture of a grizzly generally involved a team of four horsemen all using specially made lassos made from steerhide strips, first dried in the sun, then shrunk in water. Smaller strips were carefully braided into the main shanks and shrunk again.

The lassos were well greased, not only for suppleness, but also to prevent an angry,

ABOVE LEFT: When C.P. Morehouse (left) of Pasadena caught this 251-pound bluefin tuna at Catalina in 1899, he set a record that wasn't broken until 1988, when a 269-pounder was taken off Mexico. Catalina waters were rich with huge resident bluefins at the turn of the century, but no more.

ABOVE: Charles Frederick Holder of Pasadena was instrumental in founding the Tournament of Roses, the Valley Hunt Club, and the Tuna Club of Avalon. A passionate sportsman, he wrote several books on fishing and hunting in Southern California, including *Life in the Open,* a classic of area wildlife.

roped bear from drawing in both horse and rider, paw-over-paw, within whacking distance of its great claws.

Near the cattle operations, grizzlies were particularly abundant during *matanzas,* when steers were slaughtered in the open and their hides, lard, and tallow removed. In the pre–Gold Rush era, California was basically a hide-and-tallow economy, and beef had a relatively low value. Often, it was left on the ground to spoil.

At night, bears moved in on the carcasses. If a fiesta was scheduled, a grizzly hunt was arranged. A steer carcass was left as bait in a prime spot. At sunset or dawn, four trained horsemen, lassos at the ready, waited under cover of an old oak, or in brush.

At their sudden approach, a startled grizzly rose to a standing position, higher than a

An early Los Angeles baseball team shows off its new uniforms. The state's first known team, the San Francisco Eagles, was formed in 1859, and ten years later the statewide champions, from Oakland, invited the "World Champion" Cincinnati Red Stockings to play. Cincinnati won the first two games of their series 66–4 and 35–4.

Football gear in the early days, as this University of California team of 1896 demonstrates, was simplicity itself, offering not a lot of padding for the players.

horse, and fought like a pugilist, with its forepaws. In short order, one of the vaqueros had a rope around one paw. Then a second paw was ensnared. As the remarkably trained horses backed up and stretched the bear's legs apart, the riders could easily rope the remaining paws.

Eventually grounded and with all four paws stretched out, the furious bear's jaw was bound shut by a fifth horseman. Then, on either a low, two-wheeled cart or on a hide, the trussed bear was dragged to the nearest mission, presidio, or rancho to be prepared for a prime bull.

Alfred Robinson came from Massachusetts to California in 1829 to purchase hides. In writing of such a capture, he described a grizzly being dragged off to the Santa Barbara mission as "foaming with rage."

The animal was placed in a holding area of a corral or adobe-walled quadrangle, and citizens from throughout the countryside headed for the confrontation, often summoned by mission bells.

Most often, the grizzly won. But in a sense the bear could never win. There were plenty of available bulls, and if a bear killed the first one, a second was sent into battle. If the first bull won, that was the end of the show.

Sometimes, if the matchup was deemed unequal because the biggest bull available was too small and the bear too large, a fifteen- or twenty-foot chain would keep the bear partially tethered to a post.

Writers of the day observed that if the fight lasted more than a few minutes, the bulls tended to tire, and their tongues would hang out. Seeing that, a grizzly would grab it with its powerful jaw and rip it out, precipitating the bull's quick demise.

Orange County was a frequent stage for bull-and-bear fights. In a 1918 newspaper interview, a retired ranch manager, J. E. Pleasants, told of capturing bears in the 1860s for

fights at José Sepulveda's Rancho San Joaquin, at the head of Newport Bay. "I guess I was out with them a dozen times catching bears," he said. "The favorite place for roping bears was in the open country at the mouth of Limestone Canyon [where Irvine Lake is today]."

Ramon Ortega, said to be Ventura County's superstar bear roper, participated in more than two hundred grizzly ropings. Considering a horse's natural terror of an animal like a grizzly, especially an angry one, the intensity of the training can only be imagined.

It probably occurred to no one at the time, but at the very moment John Marshall found a few gold nuggets in the South Fork of the American River, on January 24, 1848, the grizzly in California was doomed. As thousands of miners from around the world stormed into California's western Sierra foothills, the huge bears were regarded as nuisances and were slaughtered for food and hide.

And by the mid-nineteenth century, there was a rising sense of indignation over the gore of the bull-and-bear fights. They faded away a few decades before the grizzly was completely gone. The last recorded bull-and-bear fight in the state was at Pala in San Diego County, in 1880.

Editorialized the San Francisco *Alta Californian,* in 1852: "They are disgraceful and revolting spectacles, offered as Sunday sports."

For the California grizzly, of course, it was much too late. Their preferred habitat lost to agricultural development, the few remaining grizzlies retreated to mountain ranges. The last known wild grizzly in the state was shot in the western Sierra Nevada foothills of Tulare County in 1922.

The last grizzly in Los Angeles County was killed in Sunland in 1917.

Hardly anyone remembers his name now. He was a long-ago Los Angeles boxing champion, known today only to boxing historians.

He was born Solomon Garcia Smith in Los Angeles in 1871, when the city's population was less than ten thousand. Little is known about his personal life, except that sometime after he began boxing professionally, in 1888, he moved to Culver City.

Tennis was already a popular sport in Southern California when members of the Las Tunas Tennis Club of San Gabriel posed for their club portrait on July 12, 1884, only seven years after the first championships were played at Wimbledon.

Solly Smith was the first Los Angeles–born world boxing champion. On October 4, 1897, in San Francisco, he defeated George Dixon to win the world featherweight championship. For Smith, it was an especially meaningful championship.

Smith's twenty-round decision victory over Dixon was a revenge win. In 1893, he'd been knocked out by Dixon in New York. After that came a long wait for another opportunity. In the meantime, Smith had gone to London in 1896 and won the British bantamweight championship by knocking out Willie Smith in the eighth round.

So confident was Solly Smith that when he arrived in England to find himself a 5-to-1 underdog, he asked the promoters, the National Sporting Club of London, for his purse in advance so he could wager it all on himself. After word got out about his bet, bookmakers, too, bet heavily on him. Odds dropped drastically. Smith knew European fighters had straight-ahead punching styles, made to order for his countering hooks and right crosses.

Smith not only made a small fortune by betting on himself, but grateful London bookmakers paid him fifty pounds each for the tip. Including Dixon, Smith fought six world champions in his career, and Dixon was the best of them.

Background: Dixon, another little-known name today, was one of boxing's greatest champions in its turn-of-the-century era. Or of any era, really. In his 1984 book, *The 100 Greatest Boxers of All Time,* Bert Randolph Sugar ranked Dixon twenty-fifth. Nat Fleischer, who published *Ring* magazine for more than fifty years, in 1958 ranked Dixon as the greatest bantamweight of all time.

When he met Dixon the second time, in Woodward's Pavilion in San Francisco, it was one of those rare matchups—two world-class fighters, both in their prime, with a championship at stake. Smith, twenty-six, was at his peak. Dixon was twenty-seven. The two little boxers fought evenly but ferociously for fifteen rounds. In the sixteenth, Smith closed Dixon's right eye with a right hand and began landing telling body punches.

The tide quickly turned for Smith in the sixteenth and he won a decision victory after twenty rounds.

Smith retired from boxing in 1902 and entered the oil business in Culver City with his brothers. He was sixty-two when he died in his sleep at his Culver City home in 1933.

In 1981, Los Angeles boxing historian David Coapman was researching Smith's life and learned that the old champion, who'd had no children, was buried in an unmarked grave at Calvary Cemetery in East Los Angeles.

He started a fund drive with some other boxing historians and raised $280 for a headstone. Today, you can find Solly Smith in the Irish-Italian section at Calvary Cemetery.

His headstone reads:

First Los Angeles Born
World Boxing Champion
Solly Smith
1871–1933


For almost ninety years, it looked as if C. P. Morehouse's record was to be the exception to the rule—the one that says records are made to be broken. And even then, it took some gerrymandering to knock him out of the record book.

C. P. Morehouse was a Pasadena sport fisherman. He was a pioneer member of one of the world's great sportfishing clubs, the Tuna Club of Avalon, founded in 1898. In the 1890s, some saltwater fishermen had discovered that there were abundant numbers of huge bluefin tuna in the waters around Catalina Island. Those who'd managed to find linen line strong enough to handle the big tuna had caught numerous bluefins in the 100-to-150-pound class.

Then in 1897, Charles F. Holder, another Pasadena fisherman, caught a 183-pounder. Holder described his catch in his classic 1911 book, *Life in the Open*. The tuna, he wrote, "towed the boat, against the boatsman's oars, ten or twelve miles in four hours."

But when Morehouse caught one in 1899 that weighed 251 pounds, it was reported around the world. The Tuna Club, America's oldest sportfishing club, kept careful records, and put Morehouse's bluefin into its record book, where it remained for eighty-nine years.

Sadly, the reason that Morehouse's record lasted so long had less to do with his fishing skills than with the fact that man has been a poor steward of his marine environment for the past century.

Biologists today believe that the big bluefins that populated the waters of the Channel Islands off the Southern California coast were resident fish, as opposed to open-ocean migrators. They also believe that the tuna disappeared for several reasons, chief among them being that they were simply fished out. Some of the population may have been lost also to marine pollution.

Tuna Club records show that from 1900 through 1937 club members caught 6,407 tuna. In 1901 alone the average catch weighed 119½ pounds. And the big fish were caught both from rowboats by barefoot boys as well as from large sport boats by wealthy men.

In Morehouse's day, the huge bluefins (and also giant sea bass weighing hundreds of pounds, which have also all but vanished) were caught just off Catalina's shores. Decades later, as newer boats could travel farther and trophy fish became scarce, the waters eligible for Tuna Club record catches were extended to Mexico.

And so it was that on December 27, 1988, Tuna Club member Jim Bateman, fishing off Mexico's Guadalupe Island, caught a 269-pound bluefin on 80-pound dacron line.

And that's the story of what might be Southern California's oldest sports record, one that lasted eighty-nine years. (Actually, Morehouse is technically still a Tuna Club record holder. His 251-pound bluefin is the biggest fish ever caught by a club member on linen line, which is still used by some members.)

One morning in 1894, the Jeffries clan of Los Angeles, all ten of them, sat down together for breakfast. Jim Jeffries, the 220-pound second son, age nineteen, sat with his head down, trying to hide the welt under his right eye with his hand. So far, his parents hadn't noticed. But then he saw his mother pick up the morning newspaper, and he knew that wasn't a promising development.

He sat fearfully, waiting for the explosion. So did Jim's older brother, Jack, who also knew what was about to happen. And then it came. His mother sat bolt upright—she'd come upon an article describing how one James J. Jeffries had picked up a few hundred dollars the previous evening by knocking out an opponent at a Los Angeles prizefight club.

Jeffries's father, an evangelist, sat quietly while his wife laid down the law: their son would not box again until he was twenty-one. So those were the early ground rules for Jim Jeffries's boxing career, which reached its peak on the night of June 9, 1899, when he became the heavyweight champion of the world.

He is still, nearly a century later, Los Angeles's only heavyweight champion.

They called him "The Golden State Boilermaker," and many attributed his massive chest, shoulders, and arms to his boilermaker days at the Lacy Manufacturing Company, of Los Angeles, where he worked until he was twenty-one.

The truth is, young Jim Jeffries worked at a lot of tough jobs. Later, sportswriters would call him "Hercules" and "Atlas." As a teenager, he was 6'2" tall and weighed 220 pounds. He could run a hundred yards in eleven seconds. A favorite story of his strength told by friends in his youth was of the time he shot a deer in the mountains above Tehachapi. Jeffries field-dressed the animal, hoisted it on his shoulders, and carried it nine miles to his campsite, not once pausing for a rest.

Jim Jeffries was one of Los Angeles' first superstar athletes. In 1899, he became heavyweight champion of the world and retired undefeated six years later. At 6′2″ and 220 pounds in his prime, Jeffries could run 100 yards in 10 seconds flat.

Jeffries, who'd dropped out of high school following a fight with a teacher, was a fifteen-year-old boy among men when he found a rough-and-tumble job in a tin mine at Temecula, in Riverside County. There, he said in his old age, he was unbeaten in footraces and wrestling bouts.

When he was seventeen, the mine closed and Jeffries found work on the Santa Fe Railroad, shoveling coal on a locomotive on the Los Angeles-to-San Bernardino run. Later came the boilermaker job. And when he took a second job in a Los Angeles meat-packing plant, he more than once worked twenty-four hours nonstop.

Finally, at twenty-one, he was ready to fight.

His first gym work was at the East Side Athletic Club. He was booked to box an experienced heavyweight, Hank Griffin, at the Manitou Boxing Club in Los Angeles. For much of the bout, Griffin made the inexperienced Jeffries look silly—until the fourteenth round, when Jeffries knocked him out with one punch. Jeffries had a lot of followers in those days and for that first bout he filled an arena and earned a handsome first-bout payday, even by today's standards: $450.

He continued with his boilermaker and meat-packing jobs but began to learn boxing skills at the Los Angeles Athletic Club. There, his early coach, De Witt Van Court (years later a *Los Angeles Times* boxing columnist), foresaw a bright future for Jeffries.

Los Angeles wasn't nearly the sports town San Francisco was in those days, so after one more victory, Jeffries fought eight of his next nine fights in San Francisco, putting together a string of knockouts. He fought so often there, San Franciscans also claimed him as their own.

Jeffries had a draw with the highly regarded Joe Choynski and he knocked out the noted Australian heavyweight Peter Jackson. Choynski was one of boxing's biggest names, and Jeffries's trainer, Billy Delaney, saw the toughness of a champion in the fighter's corner that night. "Choynski hit Jeff in the mouth with a right hand that night that drove a tooth through his upper lip," Delaney said later. "I had to cut it loose with a penknife between rounds. When Jeff took that without wincing, I became all the more convinced he had championship stuff in him."

Then, in the summer of 1898, he made his debut in New York City, where he won a decision over a contender, Bob Armstrong.

Now, after just twelve fights, he was ready for the heavyweight champion of the world, Bob Fitzsimmons. A Brit by way of Australia, Fitzsimmons had taken the heavyweight title from James J. Corbett in Carson City, Nevada, in 1897. Study the old movies of that fight and you'll see a tall, muscular young man in a cap working Corbett's corner. It was Jeffries, who was one of Corbett's sparring partners.

When the Fitzsimmons-Jeffries bout was first made, first odds were heavily tilted toward Fitzsimmons, then a fighter of great stature. In addition to being the conqueror of Corbett, Fitzsimmons was also the world middleweight champion.

He was thirty-six and considered far too experienced for Jeffries, who was twenty-four. And even though he would be greatly outweighed by the massive, stronger Jeffries, he was still thought of by experts as a power hitter.

Finally, the two men climbed into the ring in New York, at the Coney Island Athletic Club, before a packed crowd of 8,174, including a small group of cheering Los Angeles fans at ringside.

And what seems decades later like a physical mismatch was exactly that, judging from accounts of the fight written that night. Jeffries, who came in at 210 pounds, seemed to dwarf the 158-pound Fitzsimmons. Jeffries dominated the action throughout, finally knocking Fitzsimmons unconscious with a left-right combination in the eleventh round.

Jeffries, who would retire as an undefeated champion in 1905, earned $17,054 that night (Fitzsimmons got $25,581), out of a purse of $85,270, a new boxing record.

But this was just the start of big paydays for the onetime Los Angeles boilermaker. He earned $300,000 as champion, including exhibitions, he said many years later.

But who knows how much more it would have been had Jeffries hidden the sports section from his mother that morning in 1894.

# 1900 TO 1909

Members of an 1887 Southern California bicycle club display their varied vehicles and medals.

J.H.ROSS

L. Kinney

**J**anuary 1, 1900. First day of a new century—a day when part of a dream came to life.¶ And Horace M. Dobbins really was a dreamer. A wealthy Pasadena bicycle enthusiast of the 1890s, Dobbins was growing weary of sharing the dirt roadways of the day with horses, mud, cows, dogs, dust, and, worst of all, automobiles. He had an idea—an elevated bikeway, from Pasadena down the Arroyo Seco to downtown Los Angeles!¶ But Dobbins did more than dream about it. He talked about it, he thought about it, he designed it, he secured political support for it— and he built it. Or part of it.¶ His plan called for a green wooden structure, officially called the Pasadena Cycleway, rising three to fifty feet above the ground, and wide enough to accommodate four bikes abreast. The route began at Dayton Street in Pasadena, just south of the Green Hotel, down an alley between Fair Oaks and Ray-

mond avenues to the Raymond Hotel near Columbia Street in Pasadena, and from there down the east side of the Arroyo Seco to the plaza at Olvera Street in Los Angeles.

At the Dayton Street cycleway entrance, a tollbooth of Moorish design was built to extract a toll from bikers: ten cents.

As construction began, the project attracted worldwide attention in newspapers and magazines. But nowhere was the excitement more intense than in Pasadena. At the time, there were about a dozen bicycle dealers in the city.

On the first day of the twentieth century, the first 1½ miles of the cycleway opened to the public.

The cycleway was greeted with great enthusiasm, but it would quickly fade away. Both Dobbins and his dream, events would soon show, were ahead of their time.

The Pasadena Cycleway died young for a number of reasons, a major one being that as popular as bicycles were in 1900—there were bicycle racing and touring clubs in virtually every city in Southern California—automobiles were rapidly becoming more popular. Potential cycleway investors were soon more interested in investing in paved streets for automobiles than cycleways.

Soon, maintenance work on the cycleway stopped, and the wooden structure fell into disrepair. Then Dobbins sold a short portion of it near the Green Hotel to the city of Pasadena, which razed it. In a few years, it was all gone.

Stanford's football team, clad in cardinal-red sweaters on a sunny, warm afternoon in Pasadena, marched east down Colorado Boulevard. Often, the football players broke into their traditional chant, "Give 'em the ax, the ax, the ax—right in the neck, the neck, the neck."

And just behind them, Michigan's football team marched along wearing blue-and-gold

LEFT: Horace M. Dobbins, founder of the Pasadena Cycleway, betrays the reason his project failed; here, he himself rides a horseless carriage on the facility he intended for bikes.

RIGHT: Pasadena Cycleway, opened to the public on January 1, 1900, stretched only a mile and a half before conflicting demands for public money caused its demise.

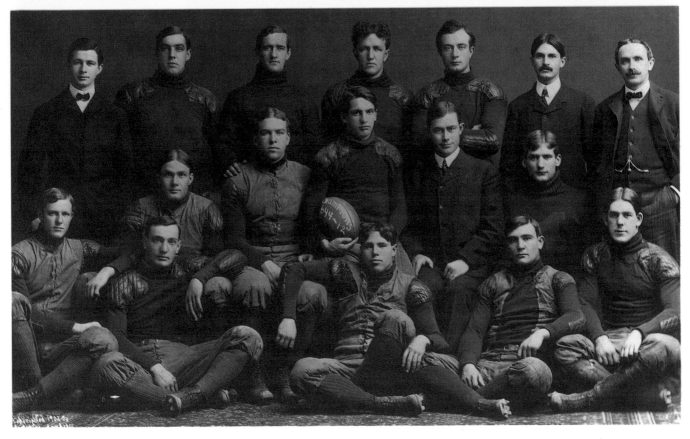

ABOVE: Old Tournament Park in Pasadena, at California and Wilson Streets, was where the Tournament of Roses New Year's Day college football games were played before there was a Rose Bowl.

BELOW: The University of Michigan team that swept Stanford 49–0 in the first Tournament of Roses football game in Pasadena went undefeated in 1901, amassing 550 points and yielding none.

sweaters. When Stanford's chant ended, Michigan's began: "Rah-Rah-Rah-Rah—Mich-i-gan Mich-i-gan Mich-i-gan—Rah-Rah-Rah-Rah."

It was Wednesday, January 1, 1902.

Players on both teams waved to the thousands of spectators lining the parade route, who urged them on with cheers. The two teams were headed for the corner of California and Wilson streets, where people were already forming lines to gain entrance to an eight thousand-seat, roofed, wooden stadium, on grounds known as Tournament Park.

Tournament Park, fourteen acres of land once known as Patton Field, was purchased by the Tournament of Roses Association for $6,300, and the land deeded to the city of Pasadena with the understanding that it would be available each January first for sports events.

The two teams were about to play the first football game associated with Pasadena's

Until the Rose Bowl was erected on trash heaps and rock piles in Arroyo Seco, the Tournament of Roses could only seat about 20,000 spectators. Opening in 1922, the new stadium more than doubled that number, which was increased to 76,000 in 1929, nearly 84,000 in 1932, and over 100,000 in 1949.

Tournament of Roses. Today, it's easy to call it the first Rose Bowl game, but no one called it that then because there was no Rose Bowl. In fact, there would be no more football games in Pasadena on New Year's Day for fourteen years, and we shall soon see why.

Excitement over the game was intense, judging from the following day's newspaper accounts. Stanford's players, who were invited to Pasadena after California declined an invitation, were lodged at the Green Hotel, where on the previous evening supporters had serenaded their team with song.

Michigan, thought by most to be a heavy favorite, stayed at the Raymond Hotel. The Wolverines that year were known as Michigan's "Point a Minute" team. They'd just completed an unbeaten, unscored-upon season. They'd averaged 50.1 points per game.

Against Stanford, that average dropped—to fifty points per game. Michigan beat Stanford so easily, 49–0, that the Tournament of Roses dropped football in favor of chariot races. Honest! In addition to a general feeling afterward that West Coast football wasn't up to the calibre of that played in the Midwest and East, the first football game also had crowd control problems.

News accounts had it that thousands of people were standing in numerous lines branching off from a single ticket gate for over an hour before the game. Soon, patience was gone. A man boosted a small boy over the fence. Then another boy was boosted over. Then a man went over. Pretty soon, thousands were climbing over the fence. It wasn't really gate-crashing, the *Los Angeles Times* reported the next day, because everyone seemed to have tickets. The *Times* reporter, in his story, made reference to "dime museum methods" of crowd control.

As for the football game, Michigan struggled in the early going, but then Willie Heston,

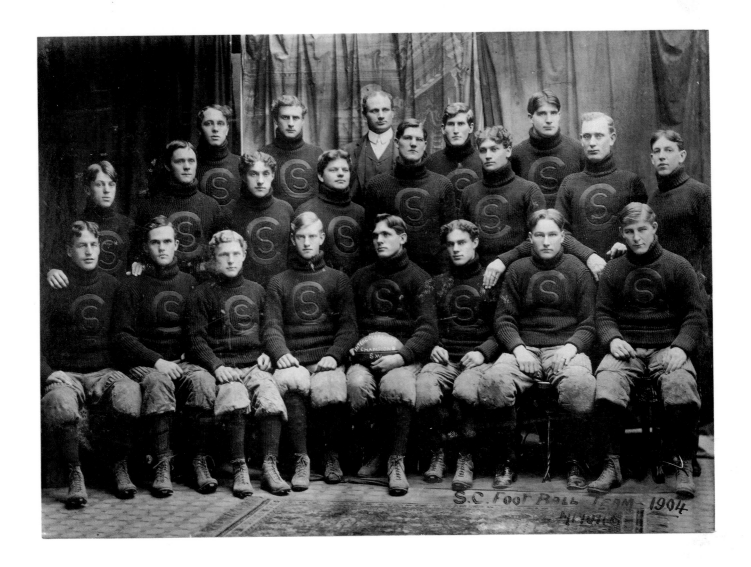

S.C. Foot Ball Team - 1904

The 1904 USC Trojans went 6–1, outscoring opponents such as Los Angeles High School, Southern California Prep, and Whittier Reform School by 199 to 27. They met their match in the Sherman Indian School of Riverside, losing 17–0.

the team's great running back, set up the first score by running twenty-five yards following a fake kick. From the Stanford five-yard-line, three plays later, the Wolverines scored and were on their way.

The Stanford Indians, according to game accounts, never penetrated Michigan's thirty-five-yard-line, couldn't stop Heston, and were in the hole all afternoon by Michigan punter Everett Sweeley, whose kicks traveled "between fifty and sixty yards throughout."

Oh, well. The game was a financial success. Attendance was eight thousand. (The *Times* writer called it "an enormous crowd.") Tournament of Roses officials later announced the game had produced a $4,000 profit.

And the weather was nice, too. And that, really, was the whole idea. The prevailing philosophy in turn-of-the-century Pasadena and every other Southern California community was boosterism. Growth was everything, civic leaders believed. Growth meant more cars and more paved streets, higher real estate prices, and more tax revenues.

In other words, let's show America that in Southern California, there is no dead of winter in the dead of winter.

Accordingly, the *Times* included in its Tournament of Roses coverage the next day this item: "This complete illustrated report of the Pasadena Tournament of Roses will be

reprinted in the Midwinter Number of *The Times*, forming the ideal reflection of a Southern California midwinter for mailing to absent friends in the frozen East."

He was the first legendary figure of auto racing, a man whose name became so familiar to Americans that it became an idiom.

For generations, traffic cops and backseat drivers said it: "Who do you think you are, Barney Oldfield?"

On November 20, 1903, Barney Oldfield came to Los Angeles, which by itself was the most exciting sports development the city had seen yet in the brand-new century.

Oldfield, you see, was the first man to travel a mile a minute. Well, OK, he was the first *American* to go a mile a minute. A Frenchman, Camille Jenatzy, was the first. He'd done it in 1899 in an electric car, but no one was splitting hairs at Agricultural Park (now Exposition Park, site of the Los Angeles Memorial Coliseum) that day.

Barney Oldfield was just about the most exciting guy anyone in old L.A. had ever seen. He was a stocky, cigar-chomping, tough-talking kind of guy who knew how to work a crowd, and there were ten thousand people there to watch him.

Barney Oldfield didn't invent the automobile, but he practically invented the racing automobile. At least, he could rev them up faster than anyone else at the turn of the century. At Agricultural Park that day, Oldfield was mayhem on wheels. He roared around a one-mile dirt track sending up rooster tails of dust in what he called his "No. 2 Bullet" in a new world record time of first 55.1 seconds, then in 55 seconds flat.

Americans were in love with fast cars in those days, and the mere thought of anyone reaching speeds like sixty miles an hour quickened heartbeats. Mile-a-minute speeds were thought of then perhaps the way we think of spacecraft speeds today.

Remember, in 1903 some folks were still riding horses.

The *Times* lead next day: "Barney Oldfield's attempt to commit suicide at Agricultural Park yesterday only resulted in a compound fracture of the world's automobile record."

The writer indicated that pandemonium reigned as Oldfield completed his first sub-

Barney Oldfield, automotive speedster, would race just about anything, even airplanes. Above he is shown in racing form in the Winton Bullet No. 2 he drove at Daytona in 1904; at right (above) as an older man, he sits again behind the wheel of his famous Ford 999, in which he thrilled race fans.

mile-a-minute run. As he described it: "It was one of those moments for which such men live. Men burst the police lines and swarmed the track, shaking his hand as he sat laughing in the car."

Oldfield, whose speed stunts began with racing bicycles as an Ohio teenager, stepped up to automobiles in 1902. His friend, Tom Cooper, suggested that the two of them look at a pair of racing cars that had been built in Detroit by one of Cooper's friends, Henry Ford.

Neither car would start when Ford showed them to Oldfield and Cooper and, disgusted, he sold them both for $800.

Oldfield was on his way. He knew immediately that Americans would pay to see him drive at high speeds. Ford himself watched Oldfield practice speed runs in one of the cars and cautioned Oldfield to exercise more caution. Retorted Oldfield, "I'd rather be dead than broke."

After his Los Angeles heroics, Oldfield became something of a rogue in auto racing, barnstorming at county and state fairs across the country, setting numerous "world records" —as long as Cooper or some other close associate was manning the stopwatch.

He was sixty-eight when he died at his Beverly Hills home in 1946.


Sixty-five years later, the old men seated around the table remembered the game.

They remembered the morning, afternoon, and night of April 15, 1905, when the Fullerton High School baseball team rode a mule-drawn wagon over a rutted dirt road to Santa Ana. Oddly, sixty-five years later, they all remembered the towering sunflowers that lined the rural Orange County road that day, sunflowers that Hollis Knowlton recalled "were higher than your hat."

They also remembered their eighteen-year-old pitcher, Walter Johnson. He was 6'2" tall, weighed 180 pounds, and had arms that seemingly hung to his knees. He could also nearly throw a baseball through a brick wall.

Yes, he was *that* Walter Johnson, "The Big Train," as he was known years later, when he was the greatest pitcher in the major leagues.

At the end of the Fullerton team's three-hour wagon ride to Santa Ana High School that day, the two baseball teams squared off. They played...and played...and played....

After fifteen scoreless innings, the game was called because of darkness. Walter Johnson had struck out twenty-seven hitters. Johnson walked four batters, gave up five singles and two doubles. It would become, as Walter Johnson's fame in the major leagues grew in later years, just about the most memorable high school baseball game ever played in Southern California.

In 1970, a reporter discovered that a half-dozen of Johnson's old teammates still lived in the Fullerton area. They were brought together in a conference room and asked to tell what they remembered of their pitcher.

"The trouble with Walter was, we didn't have a catcher who could handle that fastball of his," said Bob McFadden, eighty-three. "We finally found a grammar school kid, Roy Collins, who could catch it most of the time. So he became our catcher.

"Walter was a tall, rawboned kid with long arms and he had that terrific fastball. We knew in those days what a great pitcher he was, but as far as thinking he'd pitch in the major leagues some day—we didn't think of that. The big leagues were another world away. That was make-believe."

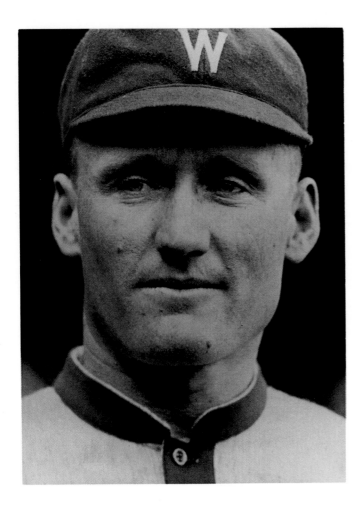

Recalled Rufus Porter, eighty-one, the first baseman of the '05 Fullerton team: "There were about sixty students at Fullerton High then. We were in no league, and we had no coach. We played Anaheim, Orange, Santa Ana, Pomona, and some schools in Long Beach. I remember Walter's long arms, and his long fingers. He threw that ball like a bullet."

C. Stanley Chapman, at eighty-one, remembered the Hall of Famer-to-be as an unflappable teenager.

"He was a very easygoing boy," he said. "It was one of the reasons, I think, why he became what he did. He was always comfortable in any situation, and he never got excited about anything."

The old men that afternoon in 1970 all clearly remembered one other thing about Walter Johnson—the black mare he rode bareback from Olinda to Fullerton High each morning. Olinda was an oil boomtown a few miles outside Fullerton, where his father was an oil-field roustabout.

Johnson played just that one season for Fullerton High. His father, chasing another oil boom, moved his family to Idaho that summer. There, Johnson was signed by a Washington Senators scout.

In 1907, he was brought up to the major leagues, where he stayed for twenty-one years. He won 416 games and struck out 3,508 hitters. In 1913, he was 36–7 and had an earned run average of 1.09.

His old high school chums survived him by many years. Johnson developed a brain tumor in the mid-1940s and died, at fifty-nine, in 1946.

Teammate Hollis Knowlton fought in Europe in World War I. When he returned to New York in 1918, he bought a one-way train ticket across the country to Fullerton. But he chose a route through Philadelphia, where he allowed himself a day to watch Walter Johnson pitch against the Philadelphia Athletics.

"He beat them that day, and I jumped down on the field afterward and tried to get his attention," said Knowlton. "There were a lot of people around him, but I kept yelling 'Hey, Walt!' He looked toward me and said, 'I hear my old friend Hollis Knowlton, but I can't see him.'

"We went to his house for dinner that night, and we talked a long time about the old Fullerton days.

"He never forgot me."

After Michigan routed Stanford in 1902 at the Tournament of Roses' first football game, tournament officials decided to rethink the whole idea of making an annual East-West football game a yearly part of the pageant.

They decided to drop football in favor of chariot racing. And ostrich races. And polo matches. And elephant races.

It's difficult to imagine today, particularly when viewing a 104,000-plus crowd in the Rose Bowl on New Year's Day, but chariot races at old Tournament Park in Pasadena were a big hit. The idea is attributed to Charles F. Holder, one of the founders of the Tournament of Roses. It's believed that he was inspired by the chariot races described in the best-selling novel of the day, *Ben Hur.*

So it was good-bye football, hello Roman-style chariots pulled by powerful, fast teams of four horses and driven by helmeted, toga-clad, centurionlike men cracking whips. For twelve years, Pasadena was known as the home of big-league chariot racing, not football.

Before football took hold at the Tournament of Roses in 1916, Charles F. Holder promoted the idea of chariot races on New Year's Day. Four-horse teams, guided by modern-day "centurions," went all out to please the fans. But the cost of maintaining the teams limited competition, and by 1915 the old-time sport went back into the history books.

In the first race, in 1904, El Monte horseman Mac Wiggins defeated Pasadenan Ed Off in the final race, and at least the *Los Angeles Times* reporter seemed to think it was a far better show than a football game. In describing the stretch run of the one-mile dirt track final race, he wrote: "Off slashed out with his whip and gave his grays their heads. They laid down to it as though they would tear their hearts out. The dash, the streaming togas, the furious rush of the horses was a magnificent sight."

In ensuing years, the expense of training and maintaining teams of racing horses increased, and chariot racers began to drop out of what had started as a select group to begin with. By 1915, the only chariot racer left who could comfortably afford the sport was wealthy Arcadia landowner Lucky Baldwin.

In other words, team owners were spending roughly $5,000 to train their animals all year for one race, in which first place was worth $1,000.

In the 1915 race, twenty-five thousand people watched Frank Lathrop win the final Tournament of Roses chariot race. The next year, New Year's Day football would return to Pasadena, and this time it would stay.

# 1910 TO 1919

In 1912 Glenn Martin pioneered air express by carrying a bundle of newspapers from Fresno to Madera, a distance of 24 miles.

ΞΕLES    Times

The Pink Sheet—4 Pages—Illustrated.

G, JULY 5, 1912.                    PRICE:    Single Copies, on Streets and Trains, 5 Cents
                                              Per Month, Per Copy, Delivered, 2½ Cents

On the afternoon of July 4, 1910, two fighters met in Reno for the heavyweight championship of the world. It wasn't much of a fight. And yet because one was white and the other black it has become, over the years, arguably the most significant sports event of the twentieth century.¶ Eighty years later, Johnson-Jeffries says much about turn-of-the-century American society, about what its men loved and what they feared.¶ They loved thirty-five-year-old Jim Jeffries, the former heavyweight champion from Los Angeles who was coming back from a six-year retirement to reclaim his title and, however reluctantly, to strike a blow for the white race.¶ They hated thirty-two-year-old Jack Johnson because he was a different kind of black man. He was independent, wealthy, didn't look at his shoes when addressing white men, and laughed while he beat up

Round 1

Dana
Photo

DANA
Photo
S.F.

ROUND 5.

HERE'S A BUNCH OF
ROOTERS ON THE
JOB

PRESENTED TO JAMES J.
JEFFRIES BY FRIENDS
PRIOR TO THE JEFFRIES-
JOHNSON CHAMPIONSHIP
FIGHT, 1910.

NOW
LISTEN

RESOLVED

THAT all of us fellows are rooting hard for you

ABOVE: Los Angeles friends of Jim Jeffries signed this card and presented it to him shortly before his 1910 fight in Reno with Jack Johnson. A big contingent of L.A. fans traveled to Reno by train to see the historic fight.

ROUND 10.

DANA Photo. S.F.

N.º 60.

N.º 54.

Seldom in boxing history has a champion employed the cunning and finesse to turn away a bigger, stronger challenger as did Jack Johnson on July 4, 1910, at Reno. Jim Jeffries, the favored challenger, was coming off a five-year retirement and was no match for the superb defensive skills of Johnson.

LEFT: Retired heavyweight Jeffries poses with a nephew a few years after his bout with Johnson.

white fighters in the ring. In 1910 America, white men deemed this unacceptable behavior by a black man.

And there was one other thing. In 1910, a black man wasn't supposed to look at a white woman, let alone marry one. But Jack Johnson not only married three white women, he flaunted them. For that, white men both hated and feared him.

Jeffries, who'd held the heavyweight title from 1899 to 1905, had run out of opponents when he retired unbeaten. Then in 1908 Johnson beat a white champion, Tommy Burns, in Australia to win the championship.

White Americans were thunderstruck, and none more so than a young novelist, Jack London, who covered the Johnson-Burns fight in Sydney for a newspaper syndicate. With his story that day London set the tone for a search for a "great white hope" who would reclaim the heavyweight title for the white race. He ended his story with: "It's up to you, Jeff!"

Almost immediately pressure mounted on Jeffries, who had never lost a fight, to launch a comeback. He was happy and fat in retirement and tried to ignore the pleas. But promoter Tex Rickard caught his ear when he advised Jeffries that he could earn more than $100,000 by fighting Johnson.

Jeffries wavered. He sought the advice of one of his first Los Angeles boxing instructors, De Witt Van Court. Van Court told him, as he wrote in *The Making of Champions in California*, "You'd be out of your mind. If you win, everyone'll say Johnson laid down for you, that he got paid off. If you lose, everyone'll say you were a fool to come back after six years."

Jim Jeffries, once thought to be an unbeatable heavyweight champion, sits dazed, exhausted, and helpless in the 15th round. His quest to separate Jack Johnson from the championship ended soon after this, for Jeffries's cornermen entered the ring after two more knockdowns, ending the fight.

Jeffries signed for the fight. Then began the herculean task of getting in fighting trim. Jeffries, who in his prime fought at 220 to 224 pounds, weighed 325 pounds about a year before the fight.

Rickard originally booked Johnson-Jeffries for San Francisco, but in mid-June, California governor James M. Gillett bowed to pressure from anti-boxing groups and kicked the fight out of California. Reno not only took the fight on 2½ weeks' notice, but built a fifteen thousand-seat wooden arena.

Jeffries entered the ring in apparently magnificent shape, without a trace of fat at his beltline and weighing a seemingly rock-hard 227 pounds. Johnson drew hisses when he entered the ring, but flashed his golden-tooth smile at the crowd and applauded—with gloves on.

It was a slaughter. Jeffries, known in his prime as having amazing foot and hand speed for a big heavyweight, was hopelessly slow against an agile, quicker challenger. Movies of the fight show Johnson in the early rounds deftly stepping backward at each Jeffries charge and, matador-style, allowing Jeffries to rush past, burning up his legs.

When it ended, in the fifteenth round, Jeffries lay sprawled on the ropes, down for the third time in the round. One eye was almost closed, his face was bloodied, and his eyes were glazed over. Johnson stood over him, grinning. Rickard, who was also the referee, stopped it just as Jeffries's cornermen came through the ropes to do the same.

A heartsick Jeffries returned to Los Angeles, richer by about $157,000, $117,000 of which came from movie rights for the fight.

Johnson, who made $180,000 from the Jeffries fight, remained the hated, defiant champion. He had a troubled life afterward, spent time in jail on a Mann Act charge, and for a while lived in exile in Europe and Mexico. He lost his championship in 1915, when he was knocked out by Jess Willard in Havana.

Jeffries lived in Burbank the rest of his life, and once promoted boxing shows there. He went broke in the 1920s over failed mining investments in Mono County, but regained much of his fortune in real estate speculation.

He died in 1953, at seventy-seven. James J. Jeffries is buried in a family plot beneath a seven-foot granite marker in Inglewood Park Cemetery. The bronze plaque on the marker reads:

James J. Jeffries
1875–1953
World's Heavyweight
Boxing Champion
from 1899 to 1905

Johnson was sixty-eight when he was killed in a North Carolina automobile accident in 1946. He was driving with a friend from Texas to New York when he lost control of his car on a curve near Franklinton, North Carolina, and crashed into a telephone pole. He's buried in Graceland Cemetery in Chicago.

He was, most folks in turn-of-the-century Santa Ana believed, some kind of a nut.

Inspired by written accounts of the Wright brothers' first flight at Kitty Hawk in 1903, young Glenn Martin decided to build airplanes. The first one, completed in 1909, required a year of labor and $2,000 worth of materials to construct.

Martin's father, C. Y. Martin, owned a Ford dealership in Santa Ana, where his son was a salesman. Young Martin had a short attention span for his father's business. But motorcycles and then airplanes—well, they were something else again.

Martin once learned that a motorcyclist had set a speed record going from Santa Ana to San Juan Capistrano. Martin found a motorcycle, souped it up, and covered the twenty-five-mile distance in twenty-six minutes, a new record.

One day in 1907, a pilot in a Curtiss Pusher created great excitement by flying over Santa Ana and landing in a field outside of town. Martin and a friend, Roy Beall, a mechanic at the auto dealership, were there in minutes. Nothing like this had ever happened in Santa Ana before, and folks streamed to the field, where many of them saw their first airplane.

Martin, who as a ten-year-old in Kansas first flew and then built box kites for neighborhood kids for twenty-five cents each, was sufficiently inspired by the first airplane he'd seen to make a decision.

He would build one.

His first plane (newspaper writers called them "aeroplanes" in those days) was a monoplane powered by a fifteen-horsepower Ford engine. With the help of Beall and Martin's mother, who often held a kerosene lamp for them at night, the first plane was built in a vacant church at Second and Main streets in Santa Ana.

Martin's first flight was on August 1, 1909, over a pasture outside Santa Ana, on Irvine Ranch land at the corner of what is now Newport Boulevard and South Main Street. Before cheering spectators, Martin flew his plane one hundred feet and reached an altitude of eight feet.

Safely ashore at Avalon, having crossed 30 miles of open water from Balboa, Martin shows his plane to onlookers.

It was a humble result to follow two years of work, but Martin, at twenty-three, was no longer a nut. He was an aviation pioneer in Southern California.

There were more flights. Adjustments were made. Martin began to fly farther, longer, and higher. He flew over county fairs. From the air, he helped police find two escaped jailbirds. He helped rescue two people whose boat had sunk off Newport Beach.

At the Dominguez Air Meet near Compton in 1911, Martin won some prize money—and also a reprimand from officials for flying his plane too close to the bleachers where twenty thousand spectators watched.

By early 1912, Martin planned his greatest achievement yet—the first Southern California flight over open water, from Balboa to Catalina Island. He attached one large pontoon to his plane, a Martin Model 12 (he was now manufacturing airplanes in a leased Los Angeles warehouse). Through most of April, he practiced water takeoffs and landings in Newport Bay, using as an operations base a sandbar known today as Balboa Island. He fine-tuned his seaplane in an on-the-water shed at the foot of what is now Emerald Avenue, on Balboa Island. Martin was under some pressure, because word was out that another pilot, Frank Shaffer, was also preparing for a Catalina flight.

At the time, no one had ever covered such a distance, roughly thirty miles of open ocean, in an airplane. Glenn Curtiss, another aviation pioneer of the day, had flown fifty miles back and forth over the Atlantic City, New Jersey pier, but no one had flown in a straight line over open ocean.

Martin did, and he did it first. His date with destiny was May 10, 1912.

All morning, Martin tinkered with his Model 12, while spectators gathered. At 12:15 P.M., on Newport Bay, with several thousand people watching from shorelines and boats, Martin climbed into his frail craft, typically attired in a high-collar shirt, necktie, and coat. He had a compass strapped to one knee and a barometer to the other.

Nearly a century later, in an age when mankind sends spacecraft on voyages to places like Jupiter and Neptune, it is difficult to appreciate the exhilaration that people must have felt that day in anticipation of seeing a man fly a piece of machinery to an island in the ocean.

Surely, as Martin climbed into that little plane, someone on shore must have gazed westward to where Catalina lay behind the midday haze, and wondered: "Is it possible that this man can fly that thing over all that ocean?"

Martin nudged his throttle ahead and the little plane buzzed down the bay, took off, banked right over the Balboa peninsula, and disappeared into the morning haze. He climbed to 3,500 feet and said later that during the middle portion of his flight, he could see only blue sky above and fog below.

Just over a half-hour later, spectators lining the shores of Avalon Bay saw him suddenly appear on the horizon, like a dark, buzzing insect. Boat horns tooted, and people cheered. Elapsed time, takeoff to touchdown: thirty-seven minutes.

Martin ate a sandwich, refueled his Model 12, patched a hole on his pontoon, tightened his tie knot, and, at 5:15 P.M., took off again. This time there was a flourish. He circled over Avalon, waving good-bye as he headed back to Newport Bay.

The headline in the *Los Angeles Times* the following morning was "Santa Ana Aviator Crosses Channel in Airship."

The reporter, who called Martin's plane a "hydroaeroplane," wrote: "Today he became a mariner of the air and made history in the greatest flight ever made across water."

Martin went on to manufacture airplanes for the rest of his life. In 1917, he merged his company with the Wright brothers' operation, the resulting company becoming the Wright-Martin Aircraft Corporation.

During World War II, Martin manufactured military planes in Baltimore at a plant that at one time employed more than fifty thousand people.

He died in 1955, at sixty-nine.


In the spring of 1955, *Los Angeles Times* sportswriter Frank Finch's eye was drawn to a routine traffic accident story buried inside the paper. The article revealed that a pedestrian, Joe Rivers, age sixty-three, had been struck by a car at a crosswalk at Eleventh and Flower in downtown Los Angeles. Finch reread the item, thinking "Could this be *the* Joe Rivers?"

He called Georgia Street Receiving Hospital and asked a couple of questions.

It was *the* Joe Rivers. *The Lethal Latin. Mexican Joe.* Finch dropped by to visit Rivers, who'd suffered a broken ankle. He made an appointment for an interview a few weeks later, when Rivers would be home, healing.

But let's back up a few decades, to July 4, 1912. In the space of less than one second on that afternoon, Los Angeles–born Joe Rivers and a Danish-American named Ad Wolgast came together to produce an incident that boxing historians still talk about.

The scene was the Southland's premier fight stadium of the day, Vernon Arena. Rivers, twenty, and Wolgast, twenty-four, were meeting in a twenty-round fight for Wolgast's lightweight championship of the world. The slightly more experienced but slightly lighter (130 pounds to 132) Wolgast was deemed the favorite by most. The fight was page one news in L.A. for weeks before the fight. At one of Wolgast's workouts four days before the fight, 3,600 fight fans paid to watch.

It shaped up as a boxing classic, and indeed it was. Rivers was the handsome, stand-up boxer with movie star looks. Wolgast was the squarish, rugged charger. Both were at or near their prime. In the film of the fight, during the introductions, there is an instant of clarity to the film during which the camera catches Rivers looking to the sky, closing his eyes, taking a deep breath, and exhaling. His sculpted face seems radiant.

For twelve rounds, the two little warriors fought savagely. After twelve, boxing journalists later agreed, it was as thrilling a contest as anyone had seen.

Then it came, just a tick in time, but one of the century's great sports moments. At nearly the end of the thirteenth round, both men landed lethal blows simultaneously. Rivers,

WORLDS CHAMPIONSHIP CONTEST — WON BY RITCHIE — NOVEMBER 28TH 1912.

Ad Wolgast's face is distorted by Willie Ritchie's stiff jab in their 1912 fight at Colma, California. Ritchie won on a foul in the 16th round and captured the world lightweight championship, less than five months after Wolgast had won it.

his back to the ropes, landed a vicious right to Wolgast's midsection at the precise instant that Wolgast buried his left fist in Rivers's groin.

Rivers went down first, clutching his groin. Then Wolgast fell on top of him. In the immediate aftermath, it seemed that most spectators were under the impression that Rivers had been fouled. But not to the referee, Jack Welsh, who did nothing at first. Then he helped Wolgast to his feet. Then he almost casually waved off Wolgast, indicating that the fight was over and Wolgast the winner.

Rivers, still on the floor in agony, howled in protest with his cornermen.

Many at ringside howled in protest, too. Some angry Rivers partisans tried to storm the ring. Welsh somehow managed to disappear in the pandemonium and left the arena alive.

It went into the history books as boxing's only "Double Knockout Fight," made even more famous years later when Ripley revived it by including it in his syndicated "Believe It or Not" newspaper feature.

That was as close as Joe Rivers ever came to being a champion. He fought for thirteen more years, retiring in 1925 after earning—and spending—about $230,000.

Joe Rivers. He had it all. In 1915 he bought a $7,500 Simplex touring car, with "J. R." etched in the doors. He paid $3,000 for a diamond ring. He owned forty-six suits. He built a two-story house for his mother at 709 Solano Avenue, which still stands today, freshly painted, near Dodger Stadium.

In Los Angeles, just about everyone knew who Joe Rivers was. But as the years rolled by, the gloss faded.

Finch, after the 1955 crosswalk accident, found Rivers living in a tiny, windowless room on West Second Street. An unshaded light bulb dangled by a cord from the ceiling.

Rivers seemed to enjoy talking about the Wolgast fight and he talked about his life's forty-three years after the double knockout fight.

Finch asked him where all the money had gone.

"Who knows?" Rivers said. "I spent it. I was a kid. Thought I'd be makin' it all my life. Spent it like a drunken sailor."

The only possession of value Rivers had, Finch discovered, was a two-hundred-year-old violin, which he played daily. He spoke proudly of his father, a man who had spoken four languages and taught music.

Joe Rivers told Finch that his real name was José Ybarra, and that he was not of Mexican descent but was instead the purest kind of Californian—of Spanish-Indian descent, and at least a fourth-generation Californian.

"I guess I had a million friends," he said. "Gone now, most of them. The others—they just don't seem to drop around much anymore."

Joe Rivers died on June 25, 1957, two years after his old foe, Wolgast, died in a state mental hospital.

Rivers lies today in an open, breezy area of Calvary Cemetery in East Los Angeles. The wind, blowing through nearby leafy trees, makes a soft, pleasant sound, and makes you want to linger.

His simple, flat, granite headstone reads:

Joseph Y. Rivers
1892–1957
One of Boxing's Greats


The coal-black eyes in the photograph look out at you from a distant past. The face is lean, framed by jug ears.

In 1913, everyone in Los Angeles agreed, Albert Ray was on his way to the Olympic Games. And he seemed to be, except that Ray and a lot of other American athletes were cheated by history. A world war broke out in Europe, and the 1916 Olympics were canceled.

Albert Ray was a Pima Indian, a student at the Sherman Indian Institute in Riverside. And Albert Ray could run like the wind, all day long it seemed. So could his friends. In the space of three months in 1913, Ray and his Sherman teammates dominated two prestigious long distance races, the Los Angeles Athletic Club Marathon and the *Los Angeles Times* Marathon. Actually, they were ten-mile races through the streets of Los Angeles, but in those days all long races were called marathons.

On February 22, 1913, Ray won the Los Angeles Athletic Club ten-miler, which began on Olive Street at the Athletic Club and finished on the Bovard Field track at the University

Though fewer runners were competing in marathons eighty years ago, news of a victory earned banner headlines.

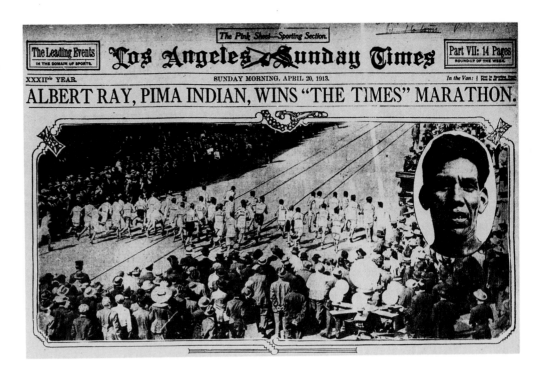

ALBERT RAY, PIMA INDIAN, WINS "THE TIMES" MARATHON.

of Southern California. Ray was so far in front of the field at one point that he strayed off the course, and had to run two extra laps at Bovard Field to make up for it, yet still won the race by over 1½ minutes. A Sherman classmate, Philip Zeyouma, was second.

The writer who covered the race for the *Los Angeles Times* wrote that Ray "proved beyond doubt that he is the greatest long-distance runner in the history of athletes in Southern California."

Then came the *Los Angeles Times* race, on April 19, 1913. And an eight-column headline the next morning read: "Albert Ray, Pima Indian, Wins the Times Marathon."

A writer covering the race for *Mercury*, the Los Angeles Athletic Club magazine, wrote: "It seems certain that he [Ray] is the greatest marathoner of his time."

Equally startling to the thousands of people who lined downtown L.A. streets that afternoon to watch was the fact that Sherman runners finished first through seventh. Or, as the *Mercury* writer put it: "George B. Haggart of the LAAC was the first white man to finish."

The race course, ten miles long, began in front of the *Times* building on First Street, went up Broadway to Sunset Boulevard and from there to Hollywood and back. Crowds lined the streets all the way.

Ray came bounding down Broadway to the finish tape all alone, and finished before anyone else was in sight. His time was 54:28⅘, 38 seconds ahead of his Sherman classmate Guy Maktima. Then came five Sherman Indian runners: Charles Seonia, Adolpi Tomp, Philip Zeyouma, Peter Regay, and Louis Rainbow.

"Seven little braves," the *Times* writer, Harry Carr, called them, in a story pegged largely to a racial theme.

He also wrote: "When the runners line up at the next Olympic games in Berlin for the marathon, one will be a little, dark-skinned Pima buck from the Sherman Institute at Riverside."

In the summer of 1989, the author called the Sherman Institute in Riverside, and inquired if archival material existed there that would indicate what became of Albert Ray.

Sadly, no one there had ever heard his name.

A call to the Pima Tribal Headquarters in Arizona was directed to Elinor Whittier, a Pima library researcher. She was able to provide the ending to the story.

Albert Ray was killed in action in France during World War I.


In the second decade of the twentieth century, Indianapolis wasn't yet the auto racing capital of America. Southern California was. The biggest race of the era was the Vanderbilt Cup race, run on an eight-mile course on Santa Monica's streets.

The automobile was still thought of as a wonder, a modern miracle, and tens of thousands of Southern Californians lined streets, tracks, and roadways to watch races at Santa Monica, Corona, and at the new wooden-tracked Motordrome, at Playa del Rey.

For the racing season of 1914, a grudge match was shaping up for the Vanderbilt race at Santa Monica between the two biggest names in racing, Ralph DePalma and the man who all but invented the sport, Barney Oldfield.

Motor-sports historians today still consider the DePalma-Oldfield finish at the 1914 Vanderbilt one of the greatest finishes in the sport's history.

Early in 1913, the Mercer Automobile Company decided to build three racing cars. DePalma was hired to build the cars and captain a three-driver team. DePalma and two other drivers spent nearly a year building the three cars.

Then DePalma was informed that his rival, Oldfield, had also been hired as a driver and that DePalma would have to fire one of his drivers. He quit.

The Vanderbilt was coming up, and Oldfield was already making practice runs in a car built by a now-angry DePalma, who had no car. So DePalma contacted a New Jersey man, E. J. Schroeder, who owned what remained of a Mercedes Grey Ghost that DePalma had crashed in Milwaukee in 1912.

The car was in fixable shape, and DePalma fixed it. And he headed for Santa Monica.

Practice runs began February 13, and Oldfield promptly ran a lap over the eight-mile course in six minutes flat. News of the Oldfield-DePalma feud was out, and Oldfield boasted: "I'll run DePalma clear off the course."

When the gun sounded for the start of the race, on February 26, 1914, Oldfield was a 3–1 favorite. DePalma had had all kinds of trouble with his Mercedes in practice runs, and his cause seemed hopeless.

DePalma drove carefully for the first two-thirds of the race, watching other cars drop out. Halfway through, only eight of the original fifteen cars remained. When Oldfield pulled out of his last pit stop, he was in fifth place, DePalma second. But Oldfield's Mercer was the fastest car in the field, and it began passing the others quickly.

Meanwhile, DePalma had taken the lead from Gil Anderson's Stutz. Oldfield gained, and soon it was DePalma and Oldfield, one-two, flying down the straights at over one hundred miles an hour. Oldfield got close enough to DePalma for the leader to notice that Oldfield's left front tire was falling apart. He also knew that Oldfield knew it. And he also knew that Oldfield would not stop for a new one, not this close to the finish.

DePalma hatched a scheme. Making sure that Oldfield saw him, DePalma signaled to his pit crew that he had to come in for oil. He started to slow down, falling two hundred yards behind Oldfield, who figured it was his lucky day. He slowed, too, to pull in for a new tire.

DePalma, of course, never stopped. He hung behind a turn, allowing Oldfield to go out of sight. Then he hit the accelerator, raced around the turn...and passed Oldfield at full speed as he was pulling into his pit!

It was a sucker play, and Oldfield bought it. The Grey Ghost was out of sight by the time Oldfield was back on the course, and DePalma won easily, averaging 75.5 miles an hour.

DePalma went on to one of the great careers in racing. In the 1920s, auto companies paid him $2,500 a week for consultant work and speaking engagements. He retired from driving in 1934, having won 2,557 races in 27 years, including the 1915 Indianapolis 500.

He died on March 30, 1956, at seventy-three, at his South Pasadena home. He was buried in Holy Cross Cemetery.

On the afternoon of December 22, 1915, Brown University's football team marched with the entire student body from its campus in Providence, Rhode Island, to the city's Union Station. There, with the chants of a thousand students ringing in their ears, they began a cross-country journey.

The Associated Press reported that day that Brown was undertaking the longest journey ever by a college athletic team. Unbeaten Brown was on its way to Pasadena to play another unbeaten, Washington State.

The Tournament of Roses Association had recently decided to resurrect college football as the featured sports presentation of its annual pageant. From 1904 through 1915, chariot races had been spotlighted, an event that had become increasingly expensive and dangerous.

Further, the timing seemed right to put together another east-west football confrontation. Washington State, under its colorful, eccentric coach, William "Lonestar" Dietz, had beaten six northwest teams by an aggregate score of 180–10. Up and down the Pacific Coast, football folks wondered if at last western America had a football team that could play with eastern powers. Washington State was more than eager. The school agreed to come to Pasadena for expenses only. Brown was paid $7,500.

Football writers of the day agreed that the '15 Washington State team was the best team ever developed in the west, but did that mean they could play with midwestern or eastern powers? Anticipation mounted.

In Pasadena's only previous experience with college football, on New Year's Day, 1902, Michigan had slaughtered Stanford, 49–0.

Moreover, Coach Dietz was half the show. An Indian who'd played at Carlisle in Pennsylvania, he sometimes showed up for big games attired in tribal battle costume, with war paint. On other occasions, he would be clothed in a tuxedo and high silk hat. In addition, he was a well-known artist and a nationally known breeder of Russian wolfhounds.

He announced, after Washington State officials had accepted the Tournament of Roses' invitation, that he'd use part of his time in Southern California to seek an acting career.

William Dietz never became a movie star, but his crackerjack football team outclassed Brown on a rainy, muddy New Year's Day, 14–0, and West Coast football had at last gained respectability. And it happened, according to the *Los Angeles Times* reporter, before "the largest crowd that ever witnessed an athletic event in Southern California."

Referee for the game was Walter Eckersall, *Chicago Tribune* football "critic" and onetime standout quarterback at the University of Chicago. Washington State, Eckersall said afterward, was as good as any team in the country, including feared Cornell.

# 1920 TO 1929

Everyone's bigger these days, even sumo wrestlers. This group from Japan toured the U.S. in the 1920s, posing here at Gilmore Field in Hollywood in 1926.

**I**magine the moment: it's the quiet of a locker room at the Olympic Games. Two young athletes, not only from the same country but from the same city, are about to enter a boxing ring and fight each other for a gold medal.¶ It happened at the Paris Olympic Games in 1924. Jackie Fields and Joe Salas, both from Los Angeles, had each won four bouts in the featherweight class. In 1983, old Joe Salas remembered the moment: "We had to dress in the same room," he said. "When they knocked on the door to call us to fight, we looked at each other and started to cry, and we hugged each other. Ten minutes later, we were beating the hell out of each other."¶ Fields decisioned Salas and was awarded the gold medal, Salas the silver. Even more amazing, a third Los Angeles boxer, Fidel La Barba, won the flyweight-class gold medal that day, July 20,

1924. All three were members of the Los Angeles Athletic Club's boxing program.

Today, no country is permitted to enter two boxers in the same weight class in the Olympics. But until 1948 coaches had that option. At the 1924 United States Olympic team boxing trials in Boston, Salas had defeated Fields on a decision and later made the team. After the tournament, Fields was matched in a box-off against Edward Wollach, another standout in that weight class, and won a decision and a berth on the Olympic team. Two months later in Paris, in addition to his gold medal, Fields earned another distinction, one he's likely never to lose. At sixteen, he's still the youngest athlete ever to win an Olympic boxing gold medal, because the minimum age today for Olympic boxing competition is seventeen.

All three Los Angeles medalists entered pro boxing, and Fields and La Barba both won world championships. Fields was twice the world welterweight champion. Salas, troubled by hand injuries throughout his pro days, retired in 1929 with a 42–6 record. His loss to Fields in that Olympic Games gold-medal bout was the only defeat in his amateur career. La Barba, who had attended Lincoln High School in Los Angeles with Fields, went on to win the world flyweight championship in 1927. He died in 1981 at seventy-six.

In 1987, Fields and Salas died eight days apart. Fields, who was seventy-nine, died in Las Vegas, where he had been chairman of the Nevada Athletic Commission and part owner of the Tropicana Hotel. Salas, who died at eighty-three, built a house in East Los Angeles in 1932 and lived in it the rest of his life.

Sadly, their spirited combat for the 1924 gold medal destroyed a friendship. A coolness set in between the two, and never left. Said Fields in 1969: "I won decisively that day and to this day Joe has never spoken to me. I really don't know why."

Helmets flew when Red Grange's Chicago Bears took on the Los Angeles Tigers at the Coliseum, but the professional game was not seen in the stadium again for another twenty years.

Babe Ruth, the baseball record books show, hit 714 regular-season home runs in his career. But if you include the uncounted homers he hit in off-season exhibition games, his total might be close to a thousand.

For example, we know of two he hit one afternoon in Orange County in 1924.

In major league baseball's early decades, stars like Ruth, Lou Gehrig, Walter Johnson, and Ty Cobb barnstormed across America, playing all-star games with local teams. Sometimes they made more money in the off-season than in the regular season.

And along the way they played some games for charity, as was the case in Brea on the afternoon of October 31, 1924. It was an exciting week in Orange County. Not only Babe Ruth, but Walter Johnson, who'd lived near Brea and pitched for Fullerton High School in 1905, was coming home.

Babe Ruth and Walter Johnson, playing right here in Orange County? Is that possible? The Bambino in Brea? The notion rested crazily on the minds of Orange County baseball followers, like too much champagne. Remember, major league baseball was still three decades from moving to western America. There was no pro football in California. There was USC football, pro and amateur boxing, and Pacific Coast League baseball. That was about it. So we're talking excitement.

A week before the game, a writer for the *Anaheim Bulletin* wrote: "Fans are coming from all sections of Southern California to view this, the greatest athletic attraction ever offered in this county."

That was in a story under a headline that read:

"All Roads Lead to Brea for Monster Athletic Contest"

Johnson, thirty-six, was almost at the end of his playing career but nonetheless at the peak of his popularity. He'd just finished a 23–7 year and had been the pitching hero of the '24 World Series.

Ruth was twenty-nine, three years away from his epic sixty-homer season, but he'd hit 235 in the previous five seasons. Actually, his salary alone was cause for great excitement in 1924—$52,000 a year.

Three days before the Brea game, Ruth had played in a pickup game before eight thousand at Washington Park in Los Angeles, had gone 4-for-5 with no homers and had bounced a ball off an apartment building across the street during batting practice.

Two days before the Brea game came an announcement that whetted anticipation even further. Ruth would pitch for one all-star team, Johnson for the other. Before he was obtained by the New York Yankees and converted to an outfielder, Ruth had been one of baseball's best pitchers for the Boston Red Sox.

The game was sponsored by the Anaheim Elks Club, and the site was the Brea Bowl, a natural earthen amphitheater with an all-dirt ball field, owned by the Union Oil Company.

Accounts differed, but attendance was estimated at somewhere between six thousand and fifteen thousand. Tickets were $1 general admission, $2 reserved seats.

To make sure everyone got their money's worth, it appears Johnson "grooved" some pitches for his American League rival. The Babe hit two home runs that day, one of them a tape measure job. Also homering was former major leaguer "Wahoo" Sam Crawford, and a Yankee teammate of Ruth's, Bob Meusel.

Ruth pitched all nine innings, allowing six hits and one run.

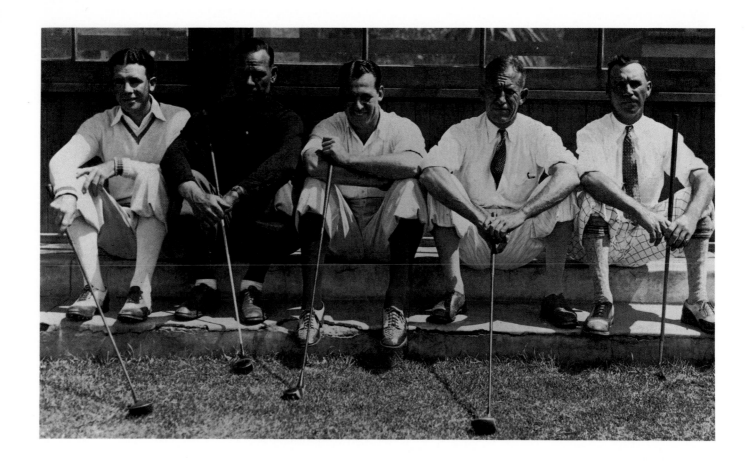

And for the record, Ruth's team beat Johnson's team, 11–1. Well, that was the *Santa Ana Register*'s score. The *Los Angeles Times* said it was 12–1.

In the winter of 1926, it *seemed* as if a deity was coming to Los Angeles. But it was only a ghost. The Galloping Ghost.

In the mid-1920s, Red Grange of Illinois was, by acclamation, the most exciting football player in the history of the game. Everywhere he played, he filled stadiums and single-handedly, it seemed, destroyed football powers like Michigan and Pennsylvania.

He came from Wheaton, Illinois, and because he had a summer job at an icehouse they called him "The Wheaton Iceman," in addition to "The Galloping Ghost."

He wasn't big, about 5′11″ tall and 175 pounds, but he was deceptively strong and combined a sprinter's speed with the agility of a gymnast. Today, they call such players impact players, but Grange's impact was historic—he took the National Football League off high school fields and put it into the major stadiums.

He'd scored thirty-one touchdowns at Illinois. On his greatest day, in 1924, he scored four touchdowns *in the first quarter* against Michigan. He returned the opening kickoff 95 yards, then had scrimmage runs of 67, 58, and 44 yards before the first quarter ended. All were broken field runs, and they were the only four times he handled the ball in the quarter. Illinois won, 39–14. Grange's numbers: he ran twenty-one times for 402 yards, 262 of them in the first quarter.

So here's a guy the NFL had pegged as a prospect. But in the 1920s good college football players didn't automatically turn pro. The NFL of the 1920s was a traveling carnival

Visiting Los Angeles in 1926 for the first National Football League game to be played in the city, Red Grange took time out for a round of golf at Lakeside Country Club. Grange, in the middle, is flanked on his right by Bill Spaulding, UCLA football coach, and on his left by Howard Jones, USC's coach.

show. Teams were in places like Pottstown, Benoit, Canton, Racine, Rock Island, and Decatur. Good players made maybe $250 per game, washed their own uniforms, and sometimes slept in the backseats of automobiles.

More than any other player, Red Grange changed all that. And the first pro football man to fully understand what Grange could do for the NFL was George Halas, the pioneering owner and coach of the Chicago Bears.

Halas, after Grange's last game for Illinois in the 1925 season, spirited him away to a secret hotel room in Chicago, negotiated with his agent for twenty-four hours straight—all this while the New York Giants, contract in hand, were frantically looking for Grange—and signed Grange to a profit-sharing contract that in its day was stupefying. With a stroke of the pen, Grange, twenty-two, was making more than Babe Ruth, who was thirty and had already hit 284 home runs.

And the Bears' return on investment was quickly forthcoming. In his first game at Wrigley Field, Grange drew thirty-six thousand—an astounding crowd for an NFL game then. A couple of weeks later, he attracted sixty-five thousand to New York's Polo Grounds.

Grange was playing brilliantly, and promoters quickly began looking for bigger stadiums. After the season, Bears' owner George Halas took his team on the road, booking games all over the country, including Los Angeles, which had a new facility—the Coliseum.

After the Coliseum game was booked, against a pickup team of West Coast graduating seniors who called themselves the Los Angeles Tigers, Red Grange became a page one story in Los Angeles. The weekend before the Bears came to Los Angeles, the Bears won a game in a little New Orleans stadium against the "All Southerns" all-star team, 14–0, and it was an eight-column headline in the *Los Angeles Times*.

And when on the following Thursday the Bears' train was greeted in Los Angeles by a mob of thousands, there was another eight-column headline. Sportswriters hung on every Grange word and followed him everywhere.

Later in the week, history was made at the Coliseum ticket booths. The lines rarely stopped, and it was clear that the crowd would be a story in itself.

Saturday, January 16, 1926. Game day. Unofficial estimates had it that seventy thousand to seventy-five thousand (the capacity then) were in the stadium, but the official paid count announced later was 65,270—not only the largest football crowd ever at the Coliseum, but the biggest crowd ever to see a pro football game in America.

So on a sunny January afternoon in Los Angeles, George Halas had proven his point— that pro football was on its way to becoming a major spectator sport in America.

Ironically, it had happened elsewhere before it happened in Los Angeles. The notion of pro football in the Coliseum was anathema to those who ran college athletics in those days, and for twenty years—until the Cleveland Rams moved to the Coliseum in 1946—they used all their influence to deny the NFL access to the Coliseum.

In fact, on the very day Grange played at the Coliseum, the University of California announced it would seek to bar any athlete from intercollegiate football who would not sign a document swearing he would not play pro football following graduation.

Oh, yes. Grange's Bears beat the Los Angeles Tigers that day, 17–7. Grange didn't break a big run, but did rush for 75 yards on sixteen carries. As it turned out, the star of the game was George Wilson of the University of Washington, known in his college days as "The Grange of the West." He ran for 157 yards on twenty-four carries.

A chance shot by a photographer stationed at the wrong end of the field caught California's Roy Riegels about to score for the opposition after recovering a fumble and mistakenly heading for his own goal line. BELOW: In despair after his error, Riegels holds his head among exhausted teammates who had tried to tackle him. The run put Georgia Tech in position to score a safety a few plays later and win the 1929 Rose Bowl.

Grange had a much better contract, though. His share of the proceeds that day came to $49,000. In his first three years with the Bears, he earned about $1 million.

On a sunny December afternoon in 1988, a bus pulled up just outside the south end of the Rose Bowl. It was a group of old gentlemen, visiting again—some possibly for the last time—the stadium where as young men thousands had cheered their feats in football.

All bore famous names in Rose Bowl lore and all had been invited to attend the dedication of a Chrysler-sponsored exhibit honoring, with brass plaques, the schools, coaches, and most valuable players of every Rose Bowl game.

Some of the old Rose Bowlers needed help getting off the bus. Some needed walkers, and some used canes. As the group was ushered slowly to a head table beneath the famous neon ROSE BOWL sign, one old man paused and looked up at the rim of the stadium.

Almost sixty years ago to the day, he'd committed one of sport's great bloopers, one that created for him a nickname he still bore at eighty-two. His name: Roy "Wrong Way" Riegels.

January 1, 1929. California vs. Georgia Tech. California's center, Roy Riegels, a junior, was a star. He was an outstanding player, one who'd already been voted captain for the following season by his teammates. To the '29 Rose Bowl game he brought everything a talented athlete could—skill, determination, preparation, and courage.

Everything but a compass.

In the second quarter, on a Georgia Tech punt return, a hard California tackle jarred the ball loose and it bounced along the ground. Racing in on the play was Riegels, who, in full stride, picked it up at the Georgia Tech thirty-two-yard line.

At first he was headed in the right direction, toward the Georgia Tech goal line. But in veering away from Tech tacklers and apparently becoming disoriented in a swirling mass of players, Riegels was suddenly running the wrong way—toward the California goal line.

He was chased all the way to the goal line by his teammate, Benny Lom, who screamed: "Stop! You're going the wrong way!" Lom caught Riegels at the one-foot line, grabbed his arm and stopped him, and Riegels finally realized what he'd done—just as he was knocked to the ground by a half-dozen Georgia Tech tacklers. A few minutes later, Lom himself was standing at the rear of the end zone to punt. His kick was blocked, Georgia Tech scored a two-point safety on the play, and it stood up as the difference in an 8–7 Georgia Tech win.

Riegels played furiously in the second half and even blocked a punt and recovered it himself. Afterward, in the locker room, years of heartbreak set in. His teammates shielded him from newspapermen.

Alabama football coach Wallace Wade wrote a piece for the *Los Angeles Times* on the game. He commented that large numbers of fans in the capacity crowd of sixty-five thousand weren't even aware Riegels was running the wrong way on the play.

In 1954, on the twenty-fifth anniversary of the game, Riegels described the instant when the truth hit him, when his teammate Lom had grabbed his arm at the one-foot line: "At that moment, if I could have dug a hole, I'd have crawled in and never appeared again."

As the years rolled by, Riegels's pain receded.

At the 1988 Chrysler exhibit dedication, several newspeople talked to Riegels. He spoke graciously, and smiled throughout the interviews. One of the questions was: "Mr. Riegels, after sixty years, what's your feeling about what happened that day?"

He responded: "To tell you the truth, I'm sick and tired of hearing about it."

# 1930 TO 1939

At the end of the 1938–39 season USC's backup quarterback in a crucial game was Doyle Nave; by the next fall he had won the starting spot, and is seen here practicing for a game against Washington State in 1939.

L ater, it was difficult to say which was greater, victory itself or victory's aftermath.¶ On November 21, 1931, USC's football team stunned Notre Dame, 16–14, at South Bend, Indiana. Most USC football historians consider that game as the university's greatest day in football.¶ But when those '31 Trojans returned to Los Angeles, they could scarcely believe what awaited them—tens of thousands of Southern Californians at the train station, including most of the USC student body, cheering their arrival.¶ A motorcade rolled from the old Santa Fe station to the steps of City Hall, where fifty thousand cheered at a welcoming rally. From there, the parade rolled south on Spring Street, then finally down Jefferson Boulevard to the campus.¶ It was a world-class victory parade through the downtown streets of Los Angeles. As the band played "Fight On!" blizzards of confetti rained down on the

waving team members, who rode in open convertibles. Police estimated that more than three hundred thousand lined the streets that day to watch. The cause of all this was a thrilling, come-from-behind, David-beats-Goliath football game at South Bend, Indiana, four days earlier.

Notre Dame, the previous winter, had lost its legendary coach, Knute Rockne, who'd died in a Kansas plane crash. But Notre Dame under new coach Hunk Anderson was still

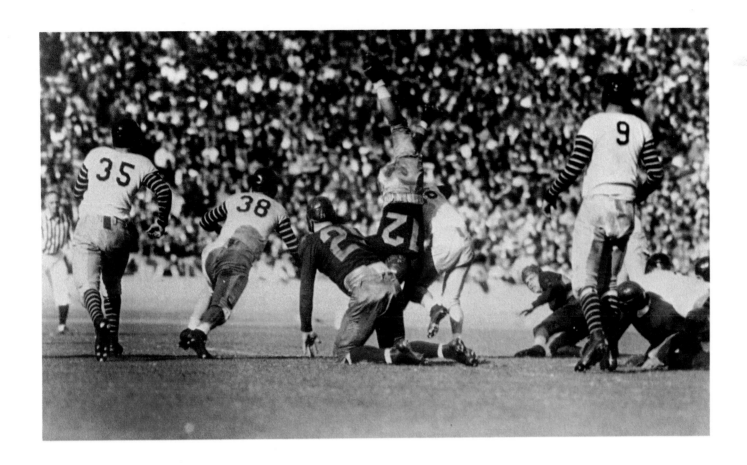

Coach Howard Jones's USC Trojans accomplished the apparently impossible in beating an undefeated Notre Dame team on their own turf by scoring 16 points in the last quarter. LEFT: On returning home, the team was accorded a huge welcome.

Notre Dame. Going into their game with USC, the Fighting Irish were on a twenty-six-game unbeaten streak and headed toward a seemingly certain national championship.

USC had lost its opening game to St. Mary's, 13–7, then won six in a row. But Notre Dame remained a huge favorite on November 21, 1931.

Several thousand people cheered the Trojans as they left Los Angeles by train on November 17. Along the way, USC's chartered train stopped for several hours in Tucson and in Hutchinson, Kansas, where Howard Jones conducted football practices. In Chicago, the Trojans checked into the Windemere Hotel.

Contrary to forecasts of stormy weather, game day was clear and crisp in South Bend. For three quarters, Notre Dame was cool and crisp, too. With backs Marchy Schwartz and Steve Banas spearheading the Irish attack, Notre Dame had methodically put up a 14–0 lead.

Then the Trojans suddenly found the right chemistry, all because their fullback, Jim Musick, broke his nose on a short gain and had to be helped from the field. The chemistry was anger, because the Trojans believed Musick had been punched in the pileup by a Notre Dame player. With their furious quarterback, Gus Shaver, whipping his players into a frothlike rage, USC went to work.

Orv Mohler replaced Musick in the lineup, but not at fullback. He became the quarterback and Shaver moved to fullback. Suddenly, USC was on fire. When the third quarter ended, USC was on the Notre Dame fourteen. The Trojans scored a minute into the final quarter, but Johnny Baker's conversion kick was blocked.

On the Trojans' next series, thanks to a pass interference call on Notre Dame and the running of Mohler and Shaver, USC reached the Notre Dame ten. From there, on a lateral

from Mohler, Shaver scored on a dive into the corner of the end zone. With Baker's conversion, it was Notre Dame 14, USC 13.

With two minutes left and USC stalled on its twenty-seven, it seemed all but over.

Then Shaver threw long to Ray Sparling, who made an acrobatic catch at the Notre Dame forty. Then Mohler fooled Notre Dame with a pass to Bob Hall at the Irish eighteen. USC had reached the Notre Dame fifteen, when Baker was summoned to kick a field goal.

And from the twenty-three, with a minute left and with Mohler holding, Baker's kick was true. USC 16, Notre Dame 14.

Babe Didrickson did it all, first starring in as many as six track and field events, winning two gold medals and a silver at the 1932 Los Angeles Olympic games, and then becoming a professional golfer. Above, she is seen with another famous "Babe" of the day, George Herman Ruth, with whom she played an exhibition round of golf in Florida in 1936.

Afterward, men and boys cried in the USC locker room. The coach, Howard Jones, had to fight back the tears. "Honestly," he said, "I'm too flabbergasted to say anything. But I'll tell you that it was the greatest team in the world. I knew I had a ball club, but the thing that pleases me was that we gave 'em fourteen points and then came back and licked 'em!"

A couple of hours later, on his greatest day, Jones did something that touched Notre Dame partisans deeply. He took his team to a South Bend cemetery, to the grave of Knute Rockne. He placed a wreath at the headstone, and his team observed a moment of silence.

The next day, the football world was still on its ear. The game had had a national impact. The radio audience had been estimated at ten million. And the USC football team was on Michigan Avenue, in Chicago, celebrating. En masse, the players walked into a haberdashery and bought new black derbies.

Then it was home to Los Angeles, to a Lindbergh-level welcome.

In the first half of twentieth-century America, in conversations about sports, when you said "The Babe" most folks assumed you were talking about Babe Ruth.

But that wasn't always the case. It could have meant Babe Didrickson, or later Babe Didrickson Zaharias.

In the early 1930s, America had never seen a woman like Babe Didrickson. She could do almost anything a man could do. She could play baseball. She could high jump. She could bowl. She could play basketball. She could play golf. She could run the hurdles.

One year, well after she was the acknowledged best-ever women's golfer, she won the

With Baron de Coubertin's ringing motto ("The important thing in the Olympic Games is not winning, but taking part. The essential thing is not conquering, but fighting well.") set out for all to read, the 1932 summer games opened at the Coliseum. Babe Didrickson took gold in the javelin and the 80-meter hurdles.

U.S. Women's Open by thirteen strokes. And that was fifteen months after doctors told her she could never play again, following major cancer surgery.

In 1950, in an Associated Press poll, she was named the greatest woman athlete of the first half of the twentieth century.

In the late 1920s and early 1930s, Babe was a well-known athlete only in Texas, particularly in her hometown, Dallas. In the 1932 AAU women's track-and-field championships, she won the team title by herself. She won the shotput, long jump, and baseball throw, defeating the twenty-two-member (and defending national champion) Illinois Athletic Club team.

Then, in the summer of 1932, she burst upon the world's stage at the 1932 Olympic Games, in Los Angeles.

Each Olympic Games has a way of being captured by one athlete. The 1912 Olympics, for example, were Jim Thorpe's Olympics. The 1936 Games were Jesse Owens's, just as the 1948 Games belonged to Bob Mathias. The Los Angeles Olympics of 1932 were Babe Didrickson's—lock, stock, and barrel.

Didrickson broke the world record and won a gold medal on her first throw (143′4″) in the javelin, and tied the world mark in her first heat (11.7 seconds) of the women's 80-meter hurdles. In the final she ran 11.6 and won another gold medal.

In the high jump, she appeared to be on the verge of a third gold medal when she tied Jean Shiley of Temple University at 5′5¼″. In a jump-off for the gold medal, both cleared the same height again, but Didrickson was suddenly disqualified by judges for "diving" over the

bar. The judges, who had said nothing about Didrickson's form *during* the competition, gave Shiley the gold, Didrickson the silver.

While journalists in Los Angeles chronicled Didrickson's athletic prowess, word reached the Coliseum press box that she could play golf, too. This prompted an invitation from several noted sports journalists—Grantland Rice, Paul Gallico, Westbrook Pegler, and Braven Dyer—to join them for a round at Brentwood Country Club the day after Didrickson's last event.

During a match play round, the 125-pound Didrickson, all four journalists later wrote, shocked all of them by outdriving them by about fifteen yards at every tee.

She became, in her time, the greatest woman golfer ever. During one stretch, she won fourteen straight women's pro tournaments. In the first two years (1949–51) of the Ladies' Professional Golfers Association, she won thirteen of the first twenty-three tournaments.

In 1938, Didrickson married a giant pro wrestler named George Zaharias, who wrestled under the name of "The Crying Greek from Cripple Creek." Zaharias's weight was held as a state secret, but Babe once whispered to a friend: "George weighs more than a perfect bowling score."

In 1956, having earned the right to be forever ranked with the twentieth century's great athletes, she showed America how to die.

Beginning in 1953, she had endured four operations for rectal cancer. When her weight dropped to less than ninety pounds after the fourth surgery, doctors told her she had no hope. According to her husband, she gave the doctors a flinty glare and said: "Well, that's the rub of the greens." Courageous to the end, she died on September 7, 1956, at forty-five.

The old champion was on his feet, dancing softly across the carpeted living room. He flicked out a tentative left jab, then a jolting jab, and followed it with a short, chopping left hook to the chin of an opponent that existed only in a fading memory.

It was Jimmy McLarnin at eighty-one, eagerly re-creating for a visitor that instant in 1933 when he became the welterweight champion of the world. He described the knockout punch, grinning happily at the memory. Then he grew silent for a few seconds, remembering the moment so long ago...remembering how good it was to be young and strong.

It was March 29, 1933. A new Ford V-8 cost $490. Three-bedroom homes in West L.A. were going for $3,200. Admission to see *King Kong* at the RKO Hillstreet was a quarter.

At Wrigley Field in Los Angeles, about fifteen thousand were on hand to watch local favorite Jimmy McLarnin, twenty-five, a decided underdog, take on the world champion. Young Corbett III, a Fresno fighter whose real name was Rafael Capabianca Giordano, hit too hard and had too much experience for McLarnin, most believed.

But McLarnin knew Young Corbett had a flaw. "Corbett had a habit of leaning forward slightly just before he threw his right hand," McLarnin told his visitor. "My plan was to look for that, let him do it a few times, sucker him in, then catch him with the left hook. And that's exactly what happened."

McLarnin, on his feet again, assumed the boxer's stance.

"In the first round, he did it a couple of times and I didn't react, so he kept doing it. I think it was the third time when I waited for it and—bing!" McLarnin snapped off a short left hook into his right palm, the impact of his fist making a loud cracking sound.

Accounts of the fight the next morning described Corbett dropping to his back like a

More than fifty years after his ring triumphs, two-time welterweight champion Jimmy McLarnin relaxes amid memories at his home in Glendale.

sack of potatoes. The champion arose shakily, and McLarnin drove him into the ropes with a volley of punches. As Corbett lay helpless against the ropes, the referee stopped the fight and raised McLarnin's hand.

The brightest part of his memory of that night, McLarnin said, was the sight of his father, Samuel McLarnin, seventy-one, at ringside. Samuel McLarnin, who'd fathered twelve children, took his family from Ireland to Canada in 1910. "My father was a beautiful man, he could do anything," his son remembered. "He could farm, he could fix shoes, he was a butcher, he could make furniture, he could run a lumber business. He had tough times in his life. It meant so much to me that he could be there that night, when I became a champion."

On Christmas Day 1934, against the spectacular backdrop of the San Gabriel Mountains, Southern California completed a linkup with its past. For the first time, the gates to Santa Anita Race Track were opened to the public.

Horse racing is probably the oldest competitive sport in California's recorded history. Written descriptions of celebrations at missions, ranchos, and presidios during Spain's 279-year presence in California, Mexico's twenty-nine years of stewardship, and well into the early decades of statehood show that horsemanship and horse racing were important to early Californians.

In California's Spanish period, skilled horsemanship was essential simply to cover the long distances that existed between the chain of Franciscan missions, then later for work on the vast cattle ranchos.

Late in the nineteenth century, horsemanship was commonly displayed at state and county fairs in both rodeos and horse races. Southern Californians were aware of important horse racing events in eastern America, too. Accounts of the Kentucky Derby, for example, were printed routinely in the *Los Angeles Times* of the 1880s.

A crowd of more than 40,000 filled the grandstand for opening day, just after Christmas, at Santa Anita, only two years after the Arcadia track was first opened.

Small, regional racetracks—many of them Spanish-style straightaways—came and went, such as the Santa Ana Race Track, which opened to great fanfare in 1890. Orange County historian Jim Sleeper has written of vigorous wagering on racehorses owned by the major rancho families, such as the Yorbas, Picos, and Sepulvedas.

Until the mid-1880s, in San Juan Capistrano you only had to go to Main Street to see horses race. They raced right through the town. But the first major horse racing figure in Southern California was E. J. "Lucky" Baldwin, a silver and gold mining millionaire San Franciscan who in 1875 purchased the Rancho Santa Anita estate for $200,000 in cash. Baldwin was a colorful rogue, known for his philandering ways with numerous women, for carrying huge sums of cash, and for always packing a revolver, no doubt to discourage spurned women from shooting at him, which happened at least once.

At the time, the property Baldwin purchased was vast rolling oaklands and included all of what is today Pasadena, Arcadia, and Monrovia. Baldwin kept adding parcels to his property until at its peak he owned virtually all of the San Gabriel Valley. The additions to the property included what is present-day Puente Hills, Rosemead, San Marino, Azusa, El Monte, Baldwin Park, and Sierra Madre.

He raised cattle and sheep; grew lush vineyards, citrus, and walnuts; and bred racehorses. He made the Baldwin estate the headquarters for his nationwide horse racing empire and by 1885 his horses were racing at every major track in America. In 1885,

Baldwin's horses won fifteen out of twenty-five races at America's premier racetrack, Saratoga. His greatest horse was Emperor of Norfolk, winner of twenty-one of twenty-nine races in 1887 and 1889. The horse earned the then stupendous sum of $79,290.

In 1907, he built a grand racetrack on the property, near where today's Santa Anita Racetrack is located. But after his death in 1909, the facility fell into disuse, principally because horse racing was declared illegal in California.

Not until Christmas Day 1934, did Southern California have a major horse racing facility. On that afternoon, they went to the post for the first time at Santa Anita Race Track, to a state-of-the-art facility built for $1 million by the Los Angeles Turf Club, an association of wealthy California investors, most notably Charles H. Strub and movie producer Hal Roach.

The original Santa Anita track was built on two hundred acres Strub and Roach purchased from the old Baldwin estate for $200,000. By opening day, they'd gone a tad over budget. Said Roach in a 1984 interview: "We had to borrow $100,000 from the bank so we'd have change to open the track."

Strub and Roach decided to open up boldly and put Santa Anita on the racing map immediately. In its first season, they established a $100,000 race, the Santa Anita Handicap, which was worth nearly three times the value of the previous year's Kentucky Derby.

Recalled longtime trainer Noble Threewitt in 1984: "You have to understand that up at Bay Meadows, we were running for $400 pots. At Santa Anita, we thought we were in heaven. Strub made racing what it is today in California."

The featured race that opening day was the $5,000 Christmas Day Stakes. By comparison, the 1986 Santa Anita Handicap was worth $1 million. The winner that first racing day, by a length, was High Glee, a three-year-old filly owned by C. V. Whitney. Attendance was thirty-nine thousand and a general admission ticket was $1. Wagering on the Christmas Day Stakes totaled $259,056. At the 1984 Santa Anita Handicap, fans wagered $1,574,708.

Within a few years, Southern California could lay claim to being the nation's horse racing capital. Del Mar Race Track opened in 1937 and Hollywood Park in 1938.

The gap had been closed. Horse racing, again, was important to Southern Californians. Somewhere, Lucky Baldwin was smiling again.

In 1935, the boxing world didn't know what to make of Joe Louis, a twenty-year-old heavyweight from Detroit who'd knocked out eleven of his fourteen opponents with an almost casual, relaxed style never before seen in the heavyweight division.

In 1935, heavyweights were expected to fight with savagery, as Jack Dempsey had, or with consummate boxing skill, as Gene Tunney and Jack Johnson had. Louis was something else. Even at twenty, he fought with coolness, at a businesslike, measured pace. And he knocked opponents stiff.

One of his early victims was Lee Ramage, a San Diego fighter who was flattened in eight rounds in Chicago late in 1934. A rematch was scheduled for Los Angeles on February 21, 1935.

The twelve thousand fans who filed into Los Angeles's old Wrigley Field that night— it was L.A.'s first outdoor fight since Jimmy McLarnin knocked out Young Corbett III in 1933 —came to inspect a championship contender. When they filed out, they knew they'd seen a champion in the making.

Versatile Jackie Robinson was a standout in football, basketball, and baseball, first at Pasadena Junior College and then at UCLA in the late 1930s and early 40s.

It ended two minutes and eleven seconds into the second round. First, Louis whacked Ramage to the body with a right hand, then put him on the seat of his pants with a following right to the chin. Ramage arose at the count of nine, and Louis soon sent him down again, for good, with a short left to the chin.

It was an impressive performance—for which he was paid $4,354—and Louis couldn't have selected a better stage. Today it's easy, in tracing Louis's career, to make a case for his Los Angeles appearance having been a launching pad to the greatest prize in sports, the heavyweight championship of the world.

There was an unusually large contingent of sportswriters in town, many from New York, and all covered the Louis fight that night and the Santa Anita Derby the following afternoon.

After Los Angeles, Louis's rise to bigger paydays was swift. Four months later, he met

Al Krueger, trailed by Duke's desperate Eric Tipton, makes a critical reception from Doyle Nave, as UCLA moves to clinch another Rose Bowl victory 7–3.

RIGHT: Krueger later played some pro ball.

Primo Carnera in New York's Yankee Stadium, demolished the 262-pound Italian in the sixth round, and earned $44,000. Finally, on June 22, 1937, Louis knocked out Jim Braddock in Chicago—and earned $102,000—to win the title he held for twelve years.

The American sports dream: a bench warmer endures an endless season. He faithfully practices every day and watches every game day. Game after game, he sits. But he believes, somehow, his day will come. Finally, the long wait ends. In crisis, he is called to battle and he achieves a great victory. There is a mighty shout, and thousands chant his name.

Once a century or so, this happens.

On January 2, 1939, destiny tapped Doyle Nave on the shoulder. He'd been at his customary post, the bench, watching unbeaten, unscored-upon, and heavily favored Duke take a 3–0 lead in the fourth quarter over his University of Southern California teammates in the Rose Bowl game.

He was twenty, a junior out of Los Angeles's Manual Arts High School, the son of a Goodyear Tire factory assembly-line worker.

At that point in his football season, Doyle Nave had played twenty-eight-and-a-half minutes, largely playing time when USC starters had put games out of reach.

USC had just reached Duke's thirty-four-yard line and were beginning to stall, with two minutes to play. The Trojans' head coach, Howard Jones, decided to give up on his starting quarterback, Grenny Lansdell.

"Nave!"

Jones told Nave to call pass plays and ordered him to "get the ball to Krueger."

Nave entered the game—and promptly got hit with a five-yard delay-of-game penalty. Then:

—On first-and-15 from Duke's thirty-nine, Nave passed to Krueger for thirteen yards.

—On second-and-2 from Duke's twenty-six, Nave passed to Krueger for nine yards.

—On first-and-10 at Duke's seventeen, a pass to Krueger lost two yards.

Second-and-12 at the Duke nineteen, forty seconds left. In the huddle, shouting to be heard above the roar of the crowd, Nave called to Krueger: "You've got to get into the end zone. Do all the faking you want because our guys are doing a great job of blocking."

Nave, behind great protection, faded back to the thirty-one-yard-line. And there was Krueger, all alone in the end zone, seemingly frozen in time. And it was so easy—a tightly spiraled pass, thrown swiftly and surely, into the soft, waiting hands of Antelope Al Krueger.

Bedlam. The Duke end zone is a mob scene of riotous Trojans. After the conversion, it's USC 7, Duke 3. USC is 5-for-5 in the Rose Bowl. In the jubilant locker room, Jones delivers an emotional speech: "We've never lost a Rose Bowl game and, by God, we never will."

Nave, who didn't have nearly enough playing time to earn a letter that season, was given one anyway. He returned the following fall and started at quarterback. In World War II, he served aboard an aircraft carrier as a Navy officer. Krueger, who earned his nickname "Antelope Al" because he was from Lancaster in the Antelope Valley, also caught a touchdown pass in the 1940 Rose Bowl game. He played two years with the Washington Redskins, then became a wartime Navy flight instructor.

A half-century after their epic Rose Bowl achievement, Nave and Krueger, in their seventies, were still celebrity-level guests at USC football games and social functions.

The Nave-to-Krueger story isn't complete without Braven Dyer's story that day. A *Los Angeles Times* sports columnist who'd covered the Trojans all year, Dyer was a Nave fan who believed he should have been playing all season, and frequently chided Jones in print for not playing him.

With four minutes left in the game, figuring the Trojans' cause was lost, Dyer left the Rose Bowl press box, went to his car, and began to drive back to the *Times* to write his story. On the radio, before he'd left the parking lot, he heard Nave's game-winning play, and heard a mighty roar rise up from the Rose Bowl.

And there's yet another story behind the story. In 1945 it came out that the decision to put Nave in the game was made by a part-time assistant coach.

With two minutes left, three USC assistant coaches in the press box, who'd been sending plays down to the sideline all afternoon, left to join the rest of the staff on the field. The only coach on the field who knew this was part-time assistant Joe Wilensky, who'd worked the sideline phone.

Wilensky, like Dyer, was a Nave man.

As the press box coaches walked out the door, Wilensky, speaking loud enough to be heard, said: "Yes, yes...I get it. I'll tell him right away." He put the phone down and yelled to assistant coach Bill Hunter: "The word is to send in Nave and have him throw to Krueger."

Why not? All Nave had done all year was throw practice balls to Krueger, who was also a sub.

Fifty years later, January 2, 1939, seems like yesterday to Nave: "In all that time, hardly a day has gone by without me thinking of that play at least once," he said.

Years before surfing became a
national pastime, pioneers at
Venice were hanging ten on long,
heavy wooden boards. The caption
for this photo, when it appeared in
July, 1939, informed the reader that
"Timing in this sport is all essential."

ABOVE: Photographer Jack A. Herod of the *Los Angeles Times* won honorable mention for press pictures for this 1939 action shot of early Los Angeles pro baseball.

LEFT: Babe Ruth and Jack Dempsey both came to Hollywood to make movies, so why not Lou Gehrig? In the late 1930s, Gehrig first screen-tested for a Tarzan role. But the New York Yankees' first baseman was eliminated after he put on the leopard skin suit. His legs, the director said, were "too ample." Then he tested for a Western and secured a role in the 1938 film, "Rawhide." Reviews were generally favorable and some saw a possible screen future for Gehrig. But he was then in the preliminary stages of amyotrophic lateral sclerosis, now known as Lou Gehrig's Disease. He died in 1941.

# 1940 TO 1949

Unquestionably the sports hero of the decade was Bob Mathias, right, a Tulare high schooler who, at age 17, won the decathlon at the 1948 Olympic Games in London with a world record total of 7,139 points.

He was purchased for $8,500 and began his racing career ignominiously as a workhorse for more illustrious thoroughbreds in the Charles Howard stable. He was trained by a Colorado cowboy named Tom Smith, won an impressive string of races, then suffered a major leg injury that looked as if it might have finished an already great career. But Seabiscuit wasn't finished. Not yet. A miracle was on its way.¶ On March 2, 1940, before seventy-four thousand at Santa Anita, the great horse, at age seven, amazed the racing world by not only winning the richest horse race in America, the $100,000 Santa Anita Handicap, but by also becoming the richest horse in thoroughbred history.¶ It was a doubly sweet day for Charles Howard. Seabiscuit's stablemate, Kayak II, was second, by a length.¶ Seabiscuit looked like he was finished one winter afternoon in 1939, when he broke

down during a Santa Anita race. The injury was a ruptured suspensory ligament, an injury racehorses rarely come back from. Seabiscuit was packed off to Howard's thoroughbred farm in Mendocino County for extended rest. Slowly the injury healed, and he went from "broken down" to "miracle horse."

But no one could see anything wrong with Seabiscuit's leg on the afternoon of March 2, 1940. Nor could his rider, Red Pollard. It was as if Seabiscuit had willed himself not to let this Santa Anita Handicap get away, as had happened in 1937 and 1938.

Do horses have courage? If they do, Seabiscuit had it in abundance that day. "The 'Biscuit" came to the head of the stretch a head in front of Whichee, and just when it seemed as if Whichee was about to pull away—well, here's how the *Times'* Paul Lowry described it: "Pollard roused his horse with the whip and the 'Biscuit, galvanized into action, leaped forward with a mighty lunge. He took the lead and was never headed again, sweeping over the wire with one of the fastest final quarters—25⅕—ever run on the American continent.... Seabiscuit's time for the mile-and-a-quarter, 2:01⅕, had been outdone by but one horse in American turf history—by Sarazen, in 1924, at 2:00⅘." Even more remarkable, Seabiscuit carried 130 pounds that day.

Victory was memorable, but no upset. He went off as a 6–5 favorite. The racing public loved Seabiscuit. The handle that day was $1,707,200, $382,700 on the Handicap alone.

Others wrote that day that when Seabiscuit entered the winner's circle after his victory, the enormous crowd tendered him the loudest ovation heard yet at the six-year-old track.

Seabiscuit and Kayak II, both owned by C.S. Howard, were early favorites at Santa Anita. The stablemates helped put the Santa Anita Handicap on the map. Kayak won in 1939, and Seabiscuit (above, right), with Kayak second, won in 1940.

The winner's circle was a familiar place for Seabiscuit before his retirement to C.S. Howard's northern California ranch, where he died in 1947.

Wrote the *Times'* Oscar Otis: "The cheering was from the heart—for the gallant old fellow is the kind of an animal that once you see him run, see him try, see that great heart of his nearly burst in an effort to get down to the wire, it stays in your heart for all time."

It was Seabiscuit's final run. Two weeks later, Smith noticed the great horse was favoring the previously injured leg during a morning walk-around. With the horse having already won an all-time record $437,730, Howard put him out to stud at Ridgewood Ranch in Willits, California, where he died in 1947.

Seabiscuit was buried in an unmarked grave on the property, owned today by a religious organization.

In 1987 Mike Tyson came to Los Angeles for a press conference to hype his forthcoming fight with Tony Tucker in Las Vegas. Early in the proceedings, an old man in a wheelchair was wheeled into the room and placed at a table. He was very ill, unable to speak above a whisper. Tyson, seeing him, came to the table and sat next to the old man, while aides to the heavyweight champion motioned for others to leave the area, so the two could be alone.

With his arm on the back of the old man's wheelchair, Tyson talked softly into his ear.

Hammerin' Henry Armstrong (at left in both pictures), slugs away at Ceferino Garcia during their historic March 1, 1940 fight at Gilmore Stadium in Hollywood. Armstrong, trying to win his fourth world title (he had held the featherweight, welterweight, and lightweight championships), fought to a 10-round draw with Garcia, who retained his middleweight crown. Armstrong had come into the bout at 141 pounds to Garcia's 153½.

After several minutes, with Tyson doing almost all the talking, he patted the old man on the back, shook his hand, then sat by him, quietly.

During their conversation, many in the room wondered who the old man was. He was one of boxing's legends—"Hammerin' Henry" Armstrong. Tyson, an ardent student of boxing's past, had as a teenager watched films of many of Armstrong's fights.

In his 1984 book, *The 100 Greatest Boxers of All Time*, Burt Randolph Sugar ranked Sugar Ray Robinson as boxing's greatest-ever performer. Ranked number two was Henry Armstrong, the 1930s Los Angeles battler who once held three "unfragmented" championships simultaneously.

In a sport saddled today by up to seventeen weight classes (junior-lightweight, lightweight, super-lightweight, etc.), it's difficult to imagine one man *simultaneously* holding three "unfractured" world championships.

And on the night of March 1, 1940, at Gilmore Stadium in Hollywood, Armstrong nearly made it four championships for a career. Armstrong, who was that night still the welterweight *and* lightweight world champion, fought to a ten-round draw with Ceferino Garcia of the Philippines. Garcia's middleweight championship was at stake.

Armstrong fought Garcia the same way he'd fought everyone else, like a pit bull. His style was nonstop, face-in-your-chest punches coming from everywhere. But on this night, he lost two rounds due to head butts and missed in his only opportunity to win the middleweight championship.

In the 1930s, fighting out of Los Angeles, Armstrong slowly climbed the featherweight ranks and attracted a following. Watching Henry fight was like watching a hurricane. The guy never stopped throwing punches. He'd had eighty-six fights by the time he won his first championship, the featherweight title, in the fall of 1937.

Six months later, he won a fifteen-round decision over Barney Ross in New York to win the welterweight championship. In his next fight, on August 17, 1938, he dropped down to lightweight and took Lou Ambers's world championship.

That's three championships, no ersatz juniors or supers, held simultaneously—still one of boxing's unequaled achievements. To put it in the perspective of the 1930s, when basically only eight weight divisions—flyweight through heavyweight—were recognized, Henry Armstrong held almost half of boxing's championships.

After beating Ambers, he let one go by, relinquishing his featherweight championship. He went on to defend the welterweight title eighteen times.

Ironically, in his next fight after beating Ambers, he won a decision over Garcia in New York, when Garcia had dropped down from middleweight in a try for Armstrong's welter title.

Their rematch, on March 1, 1940, was an odd, off-weight matchup of two champions. Garcia was the middleweight champion, but he was a small middleweight. He weighed 153 pounds that day. Armstrong, at 141, wasn't even close to the welterweight limit of 147.

It was a tough, brutal fight, reflected afterward in the lumpy, discolored faces of both fighters. Armstrong's constant pressure never allowed the slightly slower Garcia to establish punching room, but Armstrong's aggressiveness cost him the fight. The referee, George Blake, the sole scorer, deducted two rounds from Armstrong's score for head butts.

Blake, who knew the crowd felt Armstrong had won, whispered "Draw" to someone and abruptly left the ring after the final bell.

Henry Armstrong died on October 22, 1988, at seventy-five. He is buried in Rosedale Cemetery in Los Angeles.

Here's a candidate for the best football game ever played by a Southern California high school athlete: Glenn Davis at South Pasadena, December 4, 1942. Would you believe three touchdowns in less than one minute? Believe it—it happened.

First, some background. Most longtime Southland sports followers know the Glenn Davis story: high school phenom at Bonita High in La Verne, All-American and Heisman Trophy winner at Army, early 1950s Los Angeles Rams receiver.

In the mid-1940s, some coaches and athletic officials at West Point believed their great halfback, Glenn Davis, was the greatest athlete ever produced in the United States. Strong talk—even for a Heisman Trophy winner.

Davis and fullback "Doc" Blanchard were the famed Mr. Inside and Mr. Outside on the great 1940s Army teams that never lost a game. During one indoor track season at Army, Davis was taken to Madison Square Garden for a meet, to run against Barney Ewell, one of America's best sprinters and later a silver medalist in the 100 meters at the London Olympic Games. In a 60-yard dash, and with no formal coaching behind him, Davis beat him.

He played on the Army baseball team, looked like a major league centerfielder, and was offered contracts by thirteen clubs. One year, after playing in the Army-Navy baseball game, he changed into a pair of borrowed track shoes, was driven to the Army-Navy track meet, and won both sprints, in 9.7 and 20.9. The Dodgers thought so highly of Davis as a centerfielder, they still pursued him when he got out of the Army, in 1950.

At West Point, all cadets were required to participate in the ten-event U.S. Military

Academy physical fitness test, consisting of events like the rope climb, 300-yard run, chin-ups, push-ups, vertical jump, and the standing long jump. In 1944 no cadet had ever scored more than 865 points in the event. Davis scored 926½. Then he did it again and boosted his score up to 962½.

Davis's Army coach, Earl "Red" Blaik, was once asked to compare Davis to another all-time All-American who was also a track star, Jim Thorpe. "You take Thorpe," Blaik told the interviewer. "I'll take Davis. In my fifty years of college football, I've seen some great players. None were better than Glenn Davis."

Said an Army teammate, Bill Yeomans, later head coach at the University of Houston: "There are words to describe how good an athlete Doc Blanchard was. There are no words to describe how good Glenn Davis was. He's still the most phenomenal athlete I ever saw."

Colonel Don Hull, who was on the West Point physical education staff in the 1940s, said in 1983: "Most of us on the staff then felt Glenn was the greatest athlete ever produced in America to that point."

None of those people, however, saw what may have been Glenn Davis's greatest day in football. It happened at South Pasadena High School on the Friday evening of December 4, 1942. Davis's unbeaten Bonita Bearcats were playing South Pasadena in a California Interscholastic Federation semifinal playoff game.

Bonita won, 41–12, and Davis, a quarterback, participated in all six touchdowns, kicked four conversions, and passed for a fifth. He gained 244 yards rushing, which doesn't include a 50-yard touchdown runback of an intercepted pass.

But here's the kicker: late in the second quarter of that game, Davis put three touchdowns on the board in less than a minute. Only one counted, however. Here's how it happened:

—Bonita, leading 21–6, reached South Pasadena's twenty-yard-line. Quarterback

Davis threw a touchdown pass to Henry Saldivar. Whoops. Bonita was offside and the ball was brought back to the twenty-five.

—On the next play, Davis passed into the end zone to Julian Ramirez. Whoops. The ball was brought back to the forty due to a clipping penalty.

—On the next play, Davis faded back to pass, found no one open, and faded even farther back. He crossed the fifty-yard-line. Then he decided to heck with a pass. He ran left, blew by a half-dozen tacklers, and streaked down on the left sideline. He cut to midfield at the ten and scored untouched. Naturally, he looked around for flags on the field. There were none. This one counted.

The following weekend, Davis led Bonita to a 39–6 win over Newport Harbor for the Southern California small schools championship. Seven months later, he was on his way to West Point.

Davis played two years for the Rams after his 1950 Army discharge. He was an explosive, exciting player, but a freak accident had deprived him of some of his great speed. When he was filming a football scene with Doc Blanchard at UCLA for the 1947 film *The Spirit of West Point*, he injured a knee while making a cut and the injury never fully healed.

"I was never the same after that," he said years later. "Really, I was a better football player my senior year at Bonita High than I was with the Rams."

Davis was special events director for the *Los Angeles Times* for twenty-seven years. He lives in the desert, about one hundred feet from the sixth tee at Old La Quinta Country Club in La Quinta. He plays golf every day and had his handicap down to six in time for his sixty-fifth birthday in late 1989.

When Dan Reeves moved his Cleveland Rams to Los Angeles in January 1946, it was the most significant franchise shift in major league sports history to that point for two reasons. First, the Rams were not some hapless band of losers, begging for a new home. They were the National Football League champions. Second, it was the first time a big league team had moved to the West Coast. Not for another twelve years would a major league sport—baseball—move west.

When he died in 1971, obituary writers wrote that Dan Reeves had been a pioneer, that he'd pioneered the establishment of major-league sports on America's west coast, when he moved his Cleveland Rams football team to Los Angeles in 1946.

But at the time he probably didn't feel like a pioneer. He probably felt like a guy jumping into a sure thing. He was moving his championship football team to a city with three million people, a 103,000-seat stadium, and no major-league pro sports teams. Surely, he must have found it hard to believe no one had gone west before.

The key factor was the Los Angeles Memorial Coliseum. Reeves believed if he could put his NFL team in the Coliseum, the Rams could in time be a gold mine, and sports historians would one day call him a genius. But if he couldn't get into the Coliseum, there was always Dallas. Just to be sure, before announcing the Cleveland-to-Los Angeles move, he quietly took an option on Dallas's Cotton Bowl.

Dan Reeves was twenty-eight when he bought the Cleveland Rams in 1941 for $125,000. He was a New York stockbroker whose father in 1940 had sold the six-hundred-store Daniel Reeves Grocery Stores chain to Safeway for $11 million. But from day one in Cleveland, he admitted many years later, his real goal was to one day put the team in Los Angeles.

For four years, the Cleveland Rams were steady money losers, much of the problem being that Reeves's first Ram teams weren't very good. However, journalists in later years came to believe that Reeves had at least slightly exaggerated his losses in Cleveland to dampen the outcry when he left. Much later, Reeves admitted he'd wanted to put an NFL team in Los Angeles as early as 1937.

Late in 1945, Reeves quietly sounded out members of the Coliseum Commission, to find out how a Coliseum lease application from an NFL team would be received. Chances were good, he decided. So on January 12, 1946, thirty-two-year-old Dan Reeves packed up and headed west.

Reeves appeared before the Coliseum Commission and got his lease. It brought to an end a successful twenty-year effort by UCLA and USC to keep pro football out of the Coliseum, dating to the day in 1926 when Red Grange drew 65,270 there to a pro pickup game.

USC and UCLA wielded considerable clout with the Coliseum Commission in those days, since they were the major tenants. In 1926, the NFL placed a team in Los Angeles and called it the Los Angeles Buccaneers. USC and UCLA kept them out of the Coliseum that one year, forcing the team to play all its games on the road. But in the case of the Rams, USC and UCLA weren't dealing with some vagabond pro team. This time, it was the NFL champions who wanted it.

The Rams had suddenly become winners in 1945, partly because they'd drafted a UCLA quarterback named Bob Waterfield. Also, the club had one of the league's best receivers in Jim Benton, and one of its best runners in Fred Gehrke. From being NFL doormats, the Rams won nine out of ten. They wound up in the 1945 NFL championship game on a frozen turf in Cleveland Municipal Stadium against the Washington Redskins.

Waterfield, on an afternoon when temperatures dropped below zero, threw two long touchdown passes and kept Washington in the hole with three great second-half punts. The Rams won, 15–14. And not one of the ticket purchasers knew they'd just seen the Rams' last game in Cleveland.

Meanwhile, in Los Angeles, folks didn't pay much attention to the NFL. In fact, football followers weren't even sure if NFL football was much better than what they already had, the Hollywood Bears and the Los Angeles Bulldogs of the Pacific Coast Football League. However, neither of those teams had been able to gain entry to the prize Reeves sought, the Coliseum. Instead, the Bulldogs and Bears played in two small stadiums, Wrigley Field and Gilmore Stadium.

Granted a lease, the Rams moved in. But they were no overnight smash hit, because Reeves's string of good luck came to an end.

The All America Football Conference decided to move in, too. Throughout the late 1940s, the Los Angeles Dons fielded generally better teams than the Rams, and they drew more people, too. In 1948, for example, the Dons averaged forty-one thousand per game, the Rams thirty-three thousand.

Reeves lost $161,000 in his first year in L.A. and $201,500 in 1947. Reeves decided to take in partners, which included millionaire contractor/oilman Edwin Pauley and Bob Hope. Years later, Reeves and Pauley would become engaged in a nasty fight over control of the franchise. But with Pauley's added financial horsepower, the Rams were able to weather losses of $253,000 in 1948 and $169,000 in 1949.

Finally, in 1950, the Rams had the Coliseum to themselves. The All America Conference –NFL merger caused the Dons to disappear. And because Reeves that year put the Rams on local television for the first time, the Rams turned the corner financially.

The club broke even that year and never lost money again. In fact, it became arguably the most successful pro sports franchise ever by the mid-1950s, when Sunday afternoon crowds of over eighty-thousand became almost routine.

In California, the very few high school track-and-field athletes who are good enough finish their seasons at the state high school meet. In the summer of 1948, Bob Mathias's prep season went a little beyond that. On August 6, 1948, Mathias finished his season on the victory stand at the Olympic Games, a gold medal around his neck.

It's still one of America's most cherished sports stories, how a big, fast seventeen-year-old kid from the San Joaquin Valley farm town of Tulare, a doctor's son, went to London, won a gold medal, then went to the White House for President Truman to shake his hand.

On November 17, 1947, Tulare High School track coach Virgil Jackson suggested to Mathias, a hurdles-sprint star the previous season, that he begin thinking about working on some other track events, like the discus, high jump, pole vault, and shotput. Two hundred thirty-two days later, Mathias won the Olympic Games decathlon.

Then there are these oddities associated with the Mathias legend, ones even Mathias himself still enjoys telling:

—Two months before the 1948 Olympic Games, Bob Mathias had never attempted a pole vault and had never seen a javelin. His coach wasn't even sure a javelin existed anywhere in Tulare County.

—Two months before the 1948 Olympic Games, Mathias had not only never competed in a decathlon, he had never competed in six of the ten events.

At the 1948 state high school meet at Berkeley, Mathias won two events, the 120-yard high hurdles, in 14.5 seconds, and the 180-yard lows, in 19.6. Then he decided he'd try to make the Olympic team.

His first decathlon was in the Pasadena Games, at the Los Angeles Memorial Coliseum, in June 1948. The meet was a qualifier for the Olympic team trials at Bloomfield, New Jersey, later that month. Mathias, competing in six of the events for the first time, won with 7,094 points, the best mark in the world since 1940.

Tulare went cuckoo. "Hey, did you hear? Doc Mathias's boy, Bob, just qualified for the Olympic trials! How about that?"

It gets better. Much better. At Bloomfield, New Jersey, in his second-ever decathlon, Mathias won with 7,224 points. He was going to the Olympics. Tulare went cuckoo again. Hundreds met him at the Visalia Airport, and there was a mini-parade led by a brass band.

In 1988, on the fortieth anniversary of his Olympic victory, Mathias talked about his London experience. "On the boat going over, I didn't even think about winning the event," he said. "There'd been a war—there hadn't been an Olympic decathlon since 1936. The coaches had no idea who was good around the world. And I still couldn't believe I'd beaten Moon Mondschein and Floyd Simmons at the trials....Mondschein was a real man. He'd been through the war in the Pacific. I was just some kid from a little farm town.

"But at the end of the first day, I was third or fourth. I hadn't fouled up. But honestly, I

For a high school boy even to compete in the decathlon, perhaps the most demanding athletic contest, much less to win the event in world class competition, is remarkable. Bob Mathias did it in London in 1948. He repeated his win four years later at the next Olympic Games in Helsinki.

still wasn't thinking in terms of winning. I never had an inkling of that. After the first day, I was really happy just knowing I wasn't going to come in last."

On day two, Mathias knew he could win after the second event, the discus. He got off the longest throw of his life by far and shot into first place. "I couldn't believe it," he said. "I had a little decathlon scoring chart in my bag and I kept adding my scores up. I couldn't believe I was in first place. I kept thinking there was a mistake somewhere."

The next event was the vault, Mathias's weakest. But he managed a decent leap of 11′6″, to maintain his lead. In the javelin, Mathias again held his own, protecting his lead.

Going into the last event, the 1,500 meters, Mathias knew he was at the threshold of an impossible dream.

"I went over the chart again and I knew if I didn't fall down, I'd win," he said.

"The race itself was like a dream. It was late at night, maybe eleven o'clock, there were only a few hundred people there, including my Mom and Dad, and it was raining softly. There were no big lights at Wembley Stadium and we were running by the trackside lights they used for dog racing....The lights were on top of eight-foot poles, so I was running alone, from misty darkness, into misty pools of light, and back into misty darkness again. The whole situation was unbelievable to me."

He was the winner. A gold medalist at seventeen.

Tulare went cuckoo again. This time, Mathias's greeting was riotous. Police had to clear crazed citizens off the Tulare Airport runway so Mathias's plane, circling overhead, could land. Bands played, and politicians made speeches. (One of them was Mayor Elmo Zumwalt, whose son, Elmo Jr., would one day become Chief of Naval Operations.)

It was a day of sirens, carbide bombs, fire whistles, car horns, firecrackers, welcome-home signs, cheering, and tears. A little town had a superstar. At home that night, Mathias literally had bruises from too many slaps on the back.

Later, Mathias became a football star at Stanford, once running a kickoff back ninety-six yards against USC. He also won the 1952 decathlon at the Helsinki Olympics, and they made a movie of his life. In Tulare, they renamed the high school football stadium after him. He also endorsed a couple of products—and for that was declared ineligible, at twenty-five, to compete in the 1956 Olympics.

He became a U.S. Congressman, serving a San Joaquin Valley district from 1967 to 1975. For seven years he ran the U.S. Olympic Training Center at Colorado Springs.

One of the few people present that cold, rainy night in London when Mathias won the gold medal was forty-five-year-old Paul Zimmerman, sports editor of the *Los Angeles Times*. He'd also covered Mathias's first decathlon, at the Pasadena Games.

Forty years later, at eighty-five, he was still calling it the story of a career. "I consider Mathias in London the most exciting story I ever covered, certainly the biggest sports story I ever wrote," Zimmerman said.

Sad to report, however, the impossible dream is beginning to fade in Tulare. In 1988, the author visited Tulare and had lunch in a coffee shop. On a hunch, he asked the teenage busboy behind the counter if he'd lived in Tulare all his life.

"Yeah," he said.

"Have you ever heard of Bob Mathias?"

"Yeah. He was a football player. They named the high school stadium after him."

At Stanford, Mathias proved his versatility by playing fullback as well as continuing to compete in various track and field events.

RIGHT: Winning one of his many singles titles, Jack Kramer beat Ted Schroeder in four sets for the Pacific Southwest championship played at Los Angeles Tennis Club.

LEFT: Four of the stars of one of the first professional tennis tours, this one organized by player Bobby Riggs, were Jack Kramer, Pancho Gonzales, Pancho Segura, and Frank Parker, who met before doing battle at the Pan-Pacific Auditorium in 1948.

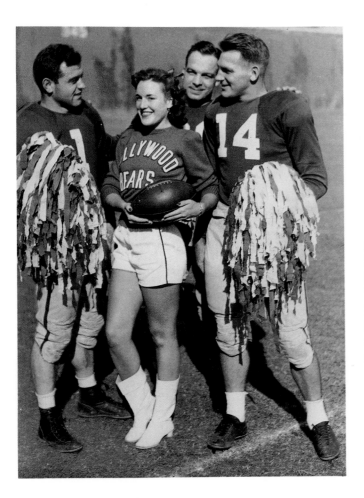

LEFT: Members of the Hollywood Bears football team cut up with a booster in a publicity shot of the 1940s. Los Angeles had two minor league pro clubs until 1946, when Cleveland Rams owner Dan Reeves moved his franchise west, the first major sports team to do so.

ABOVE: Bill Sharman, captain of the USC Trojans in 1950, was an All-America candidate at the start of a long and successful basketball career.

# PART 4

# 1950 TO 1959

Noor, the great Irish handicap horse, apparently found it difficult to take it easy even in a workout, as he shows here at Hollywood Park.

**W**hen it was over, each of the 58,730 who saw it went home believing they'd seen the greatest horse race ever. Forty years later, they still believed it.¶ For sure, it was nothing short of magnificent—two great horses, Noor and Citation, thundering along nose-and-nose for the last five-eighths of a mile at Santa Anita's San Juan Capistrano Handicap. It was March 4, 1950.¶ The Noor-Citation matchup was something of a rematch. Ten days previously, the two horses had hooked up in another duel, in the Santa Anita Handicap. In the homestretch of that one, it came down to a battle between power and pounds. That is, Citation's power and the 132 pounds he was asked to carry, against the 110 Noor was carrying.¶ Pounds won. Noor, by a length and a quarter, won in then-track-record time for the mile and a quarter, two minutes flat.¶ The weight assigned to the five-year-old

Citation caused many of the popular horse's fans to cry foul. It was a topical subject on radio sports shows and in newspaper columns for days. Racing fans wrote letters to sports editors decrying the assigned weight discrepancy.

When they met again, over a mile and three-quarters, Citation was assigned 130 pounds while Noor was raised to 117. Everyone at the San Juan Capistrano Handicap that day expected to see a great race. But no one was prepared for this—not for two of the greatest horses ever to run nose-and-nose down the backstretch, around the last turn, and down the homestretch, then come pounding to the wire in a photo finish.

Again, Noor won—by inches.

Here's how the *Times*'s Paul Lowry described it that day: "They saved the biggest thriller of the season for getaway day of the winter meeting, and a screaming, hysterical crowd of sixty thousand persons was limp and exhausted when Noor and Citation went over the line together. It was the kind of race that raised beads of perspiration on the brow, goose pimples on the neck, and set one's heart to pounding. Veteran press box reporters who generally take their thrills in stride were as weak as kittens."

Noor was credited with a new American track record of 2:52⅘, a fifth of a second off a twenty-eight-year-old world record.

Jockey Steve Brooks guided Citation into the lead at the five-eighths pole, and then Johnny Longden sent Noor after him. Noor pulled even and they remained that way for the rest of the race.

Lowry described the scene in the homestretch: "Down the track they pounded, stride for stride, rhythmic as the breakers, Citation slightly in front." Two strides from the wire, Lowry wrote, only a timely bob of Noor's head won the race.

Afterward, Longden called it his toughest race. "I have to take my hat off to Citation," he said. "He's truly great. Noor was headed in the drive to the wire, but I had a great horse under me and we had to go all out to beat a marvelous champion."

Said Brooks: "Citation ran a great race. It was certainly no disgrace to lose such a tough one to another great horse. I thought I had him beaten, but he came again at us in the last strides and nailed us at the wire."

For the Los Angeles Rams, December 24, 1951, was their finest hour in Los Angeles. And when they left Los Angeles in 1980 for Anaheim, it still was.

By 1990, the 1951 juggernaut was still the only Southern California Rams team to win a National Football League championship. On that day, under threatening skies in the Coliseum, a quarterback named Van Brocklin and an end named Fears executed a perfect play with time running out to beat the Cleveland Browns, 24–17.

And you'd figure you'd need a perfect play to beat the game's greatest quarterback, Cleveland's Otto Graham.

Nearly four decades later, more than a few pro football scholars still consider Graham football's greatest quarterback, the NFL's all-time number one winner. A look at the standings during his career tells it all: ten seasons, ten division championships, four consecutive All America Conference championships, three NFL championships. As his coach, Paul Brown, once said: "The test of a quarterback is where his team finishes. So Otto Graham, by that standard, was the best of all time."

No one had to convince the Rams. In the 1950 title game, trailing 28–27 with 1:50 to play, Graham took the Browns sixty-eight yards to the Rams' eleven, where Lou Groza kicked the winning field goal with seventeen seconds left.

For the 1951 title game, the Rams assigned two big, fast defensive ends, Andy Robustelli and Larry Brink, to put the clamps on Graham. It worked. With Robustelli and Brink hounding him all afternoon, Graham, when he wasn't sacked, several times forced passes into the hands of Ram linebackers Marv Johnson and Don Paul.

The defensive strategy worked, in the sense that the Rams were tied with the game on the line. In 1989, Tom Fears remembered the huddle when quarterback Norm Van Brocklin, who had replaced starter Bob Waterfield late in the third quarter, barked out the call. "He called a 'Red Right, X-Y Post,' which meant I was supposed to go down toward the middle of the field, fake to the right, and keep right on going. It was a deep-pass play, and when I looked back for the ball I could see it was coming right for me, but I was between the Browns' cornerback and the safety.

"Luckily for us, those two guys ran into each other and lost their balance just as I was catching a ball that was absolutely perfect—I was in full stride and it came right to my hands.

"In the end zone, I had that feeling that it was too good to be true, so right away I looked back for a flag. There weren't any."

It was a third-and-three, seventy-three-yard play, with 7:35 left. The closest the Browns could come after that was the Rams' forty-two, where rookie defensive back Norb

Norm Van Brocklin (left) and Bob Waterfield shared quarterbacking duties for the Rams in their upset of Cleveland for the 1951 NFL championship.

Hecker essentially ended Cleveland's last hope. Graham tried a pitch play on fourth-and-two from the L.A. forty-two, and Hecker threw the ballcarrier, Dubs Jones, for a two-yard loss.

Afterward, in the locker room, players and coaches were doused in the showers and by champagne. In the jubilation, no one could have known that no Ram team, not in Los Angeles or Anaheim, would experience such a moment for decades.

On the evening of June 29, 1956, about twenty thousand spectators at the U.S. Olympic team track-and-field trials in the Los Angeles Memorial Coliseum sat in tense silence, watching a pile of sawdust.

Above the sawdust was a metal black-and-white bar, a half-inch over seven feet above the ground. A tall, lean nineteen-year-old named Charlie Dumas, a Compton College freshman, approached the bar with slow, confident strides. He was attempting to jump into the unknown. No human being had ever jumped that high. As a sports barrier, seven feet had but a few seconds left.

Dumas's body, seemingly yanked upward by a mighty kick of his lead right leg, rose to the facing edge, then to the top of the bar. For an instant, his body was straight along the top of the bar. He rolled over it and began to descend into the sawdust. When he landed, spectators began leaping to their feet, cheering. They'd seen history.

But wait. The bar trembled. When Dumas landed on his back in the pit, he looked up and watched the quivering bar. It was as if fate hadn't yet decided if the young man on his back in the sawdust was worthy enough for track-and-field's history books.

The bar stopped trembling, and stayed. A human being had jumped seven feet above the surface of his planet. Seven feet in the high jump has long since lost its magic, of course.

The event was changed forever in the mid-1960s when an Oregon State jumper named Dick Fosbury figured out that it was best to go over the bar on your back, not your stomach. Also, head first, not feet first.

Even track nuts have lost count of how many men have jumped seven feet since Dumas broke the barrier, but it's well over five thousand. In a good year now, two or three dozen high school jumpers clear seven. In fact, by the late 1980s, track-and-field experts were predicting a woman would soon clear seven feet.

Dumas, who won a gold medal at the Melbourne Olympics (at 6′11½″) that summer, later competed for USC. By the late 1980s, he was in eighth place on USC's all-time high-jump list.

So folks pretty much yawn at seven today. But in the mid-1950s, seven feet in the high jump represented supreme excellence, an ultimate challenge to athletic skill and training. It was a psychological barrier that had turned away for fifteen years the assaults of such world-class jumpers as Les Steers, Walter Davis, and Ernie Shelton. All faltered. All but Dumas.

On Saturday, June 29, 1956, Marilyn Monroe married Arthur Miller. New ocean-view homes in Palos Verdes were selling for $26,525. Grauman's Chinese was showing *The King and I*. Mickey Mantle, twenty-four, was hitting .379 and leading the major leagues with twenty-seven home runs. For Charlie Dumas, the breakaway height in the Coliseum that night was 6′9½″. Dumas, Vern Wilson, and Phil Reavis all cleared the height and made the Olympic team.

Dumas asked officials to raise the bar to seven feet, one-half inch. "My first try was a miss," Dumas recalled, thirty years later. "But I felt fairly confident. There was no pressure, I knew I'd made the plane [to the Olympics]. Plus, I'd had attempts in competition at seven feet before, so I knew what it was about. Maybe I was just so relaxed, I did everything right."

Dumas put his sweat suit back on and jogged the length of the Coliseum turf, while spectators in the mostly empty Coliseum rushed down to lower rows for a better look. He sat down, pulled his sweats off, and retied the laces of his green shoes. He faced the bar again. Then he remembered the feeling, lying in the sawdust and watching the bar tremble on its pegs. "I ticked it somewhere, my foot, hand...but it stayed up. The place went wild. It was a super night."

For Dave Schwartz, the official who was running the high jump that night, the aftermath of Dumas's historic jump was a little too wild. "With Dumas and Ernie Shelton in those days, we knew we might have a seven-foot jump to handle," he said.

"We'd measured the height before he jumped, which was required for record certification. It had to be measured afterward, too. But after he cleared it, all kinds of photographers, sportswriters, and friends of Dumas's came out of nowhere. I was afraid someone would bump a standard and knock the bar off. That would have negated the jump. So we had to clear everyone away to remeasure."

Charlie Dumas, now a high school counselor in the San Fernando Valley, was born in the right era.

"The Fosbury Flop came along a few years after I got out of high jumping," he said. "I never could have mastered it. I just didn't have that kind of range of motion. And remember, we jumped into sawdust in those days.

"I would've broken my neck."

Footnote: on that night at the Coliseum, no one could have possibly imagined anyone

jumping eight feet, ever. Yet thirty-three years and thirty days later, it happened. In the summer of 1989, a Cuban, Javier Sotomayor, jumped eight feet in a meet at San Juan, Puerto Rico.

In the high school football season of 1956, Mickey Flynn of Anaheim High School and Randy Meadows of Downey High were Southern California's Touchdown Twins. Both led their teams to 12–0 records that season, going into the season's final game. And just as if some screenwriter had scripted the whole thing, they wound up playing in the California Interscholastic Federation (CIF) championship game against each other, in the Coliseum, on December 14, 1956.

No one could remember two explosive teams like these two, coming together in a championship game. And no one could remember two explosive players like these two, either. Flynn was a 5′10″, 170-pound halfback who'd been the CIF's player of the year the previous season when he'd averaged a remarkable 15.9 yards per carry and had had a run of at least 50 yards or more in every game. In 1956, he came into the Downey showdown averaging 16.1 yards per carry.

Meadows, 6′ tall and 170 pounds, had broken Marty Keough's CIF single-season scoring

USC's Charlie Dumas shows the classic high jumping form of the late 1950s, when he won the '56 Olympics and soared over 7 feet for the first time in the event's history.

record by scoring 197 points. He'd also rushed for 2,038 yards, averaging almost 16 yards per carry. Combined, Flynn and Meadows had scored eighty-eight touchdowns in three seasons.

In the playoff games the weekend prior to their title game, Flynn and Meadows heightened the anticipation. Flynn, in Anaheim's 34–6 win over San Diego Hoover, scored on sweeps measuring 57 and 20 yards in two-and-a-half quarters. Meadows, in Downey's 54–14 win over Beverly Hills, scored three times on runs of 42 and 55 yards and caught a touchdown pass on an 80-yard play. The week before, against Antelope Valley, he'd scored on runs of 75, 65, 65, and 50 yards and totaled 393 yards.

Anticipation for Anaheim-Downey rivaled that for any other previous high school football game played in Southern California. Some of the best-remembered matchups included the 1921 game between Santa Monica and Los Angeles Poly, the 1939 title game pitting Santa Barbara against Alhambra, and the 1951 Pomona-Monrovia game, when quarterback Marty Keough, led Pomona to a 26–13 win.

No one could remember two teams so evenly matched, either. Downey came into the game having scored 428 points, Anaheim 423. And it turned out they were *more* evenly matched than anyone thought. A record prep crowd of 41,383 turned out on a foggy night. Both Flynn and Meadows broke long runs, and the two teams played to a 13–13 tie.

Late in the first quarter, Flynn burst off tackle and scored on a 62-yard sprint. Two minutes later, Meadows swept around Anaheim's left side and bolted down the sideline on a 69-yard touchdown run. It was a memorable game, but one that many of the 41,383 couldn't see. The fog that rolled in and out of the Coliseum that night was so dense that fans seated in the upper rows couldn't see a thing for parts of the game.

In 1989, Mickey Flynn remembered a game played out in almost unreal circumstances. "We had a case of food poisoning on the team that week that we got from some bad barbecued chicken at a cookout," he said. "Four of the guys were so sick they rode to the Coliseum stretched out in the back of station wagons.

"The other strange thing was the fog—for a lot of the time, we couldn't see a thing on the field. For all the buildup that game had, it was really a strange night."

For Meadows, the memory of playing in the Coliseum before a big crowd, over thirty years later, has eclipsed the game itself. "I couldn't get over the feeling that night of playing in such an enormous place as the Coliseum, and listening to that big crowd," he recalled. "It was quite a night."

Neither Flynn nor Meadows developed into college football standouts, as many expected. Flynn played briefly at Long Beach City College, Arizona State, and Santa Ana College, before injuries ended his career. Meadows, who enrolled first at USC and then Long Beach City College, later enlisted in the Army and played service football in West Germany.

Both Flynn and Meadows turned fifty in 1988. Flynn, who lives in Fullerton, is a heavy-equipment operator and has been a grandfather since 1982. Meadows is a welder and lives in Hemet.

There's a Flynn-Meadows footnote to the 1956 high school football season. They teamed up in the same backfield for California's annual North-South Shrine All-Star Game at the Coliseum the following summer.

The prospect of seeing the Touchdown Twins in the same backfield drew one of the biggest high school crowds in history, 85,931, to the Coliseum on a hot July night. Unfortunately, both players fell on their faces. The no-name North team, thirteen-point underdogs, won 32–0.

Meadows gained five yards on two carries, Flynn four on three carries.

On the morning of the day major league baseball came to Los Angeles, April 18, 1958, about eight thousand people gathered in front of the Spring Street steps at Los Angeles City Hall for a welcoming ceremony.

Presently, a bus pulled up. As the uniformed Dodgers filed off the bus and trotted up the city hall steps—in their shower sandals—the L.A. Police Band struck up "California, Here I Come!" and a mighty cheer went up.

If you had to pick one twentieth-century day in Southern California that might have registered on the Richter Sports Scale, April 18, 1958, might have been the day.

This was heady stuff.

Major league baseball in Los Angeles! Talked about for decades, it was here at last. Hard to believe, but there they were—all those players with the familiar blue "Dodgers" script on their chests: Duke Snider, Don Drysdale, Wally Moon, Gil Hodges, Pee Wee Reese, and all the other names associated for so long with Ebbets Field in Brooklyn.

It was a memorable moment and, for Los Angeles and California, a landmark event. In that moment, it seemed, the United States had tilted slightly westward. The move of the

ABOVE: Here is how the Coliseum looked on opening day as it was set up for the unfamiliar sport of baseball. The Dodgers beat the Giants on that day and played four years here before moving to Chavez Ravine.

RIGHT: Wearing their locker room sandals on the unaccustomed pavement in front of City Hall, on April 18, 1958 the Dodgers make their way through a crowd of enthusiastic greeters.

Brooklyn Dodgers to Los Angeles, announced the previous October 8, along with the same-year shift of the New York Giants to San Francisco, helped give not only those two cities but western America a new identity.

As late as 1957, when rumors stirred that New York might lose the Dodgers and the Giants, two of its three major league teams, some unbelieving New York sports journalists sneered at the suggestion. The Dodgers? Move to L.A.? Whaddya, crazy?

So after Giants' owner Horace Stoneham announced on August 20, 1957, that he would move his club to San Francisco, New Yorkers were knocked for a loop. Dodgers owner Walter O'Malley, meanwhile, who had badgered New York politicians for years for a new stadium on available land in Brooklyn, now began to see action. All this was much too late, of course.

O'Malley first got everyone's attention in New York when in early 1957 he bought Los Angeles's Pacific Coast League franchise, the Angels, and its twenty-two-thousand-seat

Wrigley Field, for $2.5 million. And when Los Angeles mayor Norris Poulson flew to Vero Beach, Florida, to confer behind closed doors with O'Malley during the club's 1957 spring training season, it's believed—but never confirmed—that during that meeting a Chavez Ravine-for-Wrigley Field swap was first discussed.

Nelson Rockefeller came up with an eleventh hour, $7.5 million offer in September to start a new stadium project at Atlantic and Flatbush avenues in Brooklyn. But by then, O'Malley was deep into serious negotiations with Los Angeles industrialist Harold C. McClellan, appointed to represent the city and county of Los Angeles in negotiations with O'Malley.

The day before the move was officially announced, the last peg in the deal was pounded into place—the Los Angeles City Council, by a 10–4 vote, agreed to sell to O'Malley the three-hundred-acre Chavez Ravine tract, near downtown Los Angeles. Previously, the city had agreed to spend $2 million in street improvements. In later years, it would be called "The Treaty of Chavez Ravine."

Later, completing what was in effect a swap, O'Malley signed Wrigley Field over to the city.

The next afternoon in New York, following a Dodgers' stockholders meeting, O'Malley made the announcement. His publicity man, Red Patterson, on October 8, 1957, read the announcement to reporters at the World Series press room at the Waldorf Astoria Hotel.

At Los Angeles City Hall on the morning of April 18, 1958, after politicians made speeches, and someone put a sombrero on O'Malley's head, a parade was begun, one that took the Dodgers through downtown L.A. to the Coliseum, for their first game in Los Angeles, against San Francisco. The two teams had opened the '58 National League season at San Francisco's temporary home, Seals Stadium, and the Giants had taken two-out-of-three from the Dodgers.

The Dodgers' City Hall-to-the-Coliseum parade was described as the biggest downtown sports celebration since USC's 1931 Trojans were welcomed home from upsetting Notre Dame. Crowds spilled into the streets during the motorcade. At seventh and Broadway, crowds were so dense that the parade momentarily ground to a halt. Even when the Dodgers made it to the Harbor Freeway and proceeded toward the Coliseum, crowds lined up on the overpasses and waved to the Dodgers as they rolled by below.

Something like this had happened fifty-five years earlier. In 1903, Los Angeles, then a town of 102,000, welcomed its first Pacific Coast League team, the Looloos—honest! A reporter that day described a welcoming brass band, a parade, and finally a game, when the Looloos defeated the Seattle Webfeet, 2–1.

At 1 P.M. on April 18, 1958, the wacky, wonderful four-year history of major league baseball in the Coliseum, with its forty-two-foot-high left field screen, was under way.

In their first game in Los Angeles, the Dodgers beat the Giants, 6–5, before 78,672, the largest-ever National League crowd.

For the trivia-oriented: the winning pitcher that day was Carl Erskine; the loser, Alan Worthington. In the fourth inning, the Giants' Hank Sauer hit the first Los Angeles major league home run, a legitimate 340-footer to left-center. In the eighth, Sauer hit another one, a cheapie, over the screen. The first Dodger home run in Los Angeles? Come on now, think— you get five hundred points for this one...Dick Gray, in the seventh.

On Dodger Day One in L.A., the crowd was the page-one story. Actually, some were

Dodgers, Giants, and 78,672 paying customers pledge allegiance to the flag on opening day in one of the most unusual baseball parks in America.

disappointed. Many expected a ninety-thousand-plus turnout. The following day, attendance fell off dramatically—to 41,303, still bigger than any crowd the Dodgers had attracted in years in Brooklyn. The Dodgers, despite finishing seventh in 1958, would go on to attract 1,845,556 spectators in their first season at the Coliseum.

In 1959, their best Coliseum season, the Dodgers put some attendance records on the books that might remain as long as the game is played, or unless another team moves to the Coliseum. The club amazed everyone by not only winning the National League pennant but by beating the Chicago White Sox, four games to two, in the World Series.

All three of the Series games in the Coliseum drew over ninety-two thousand. And in that season the Dodgers and New York Yankees drew 93,103 for a benefit game for Dodger catcher Roy Campanella, paralyzed in an auto accident. It's still the all-time record baseball crowd.

By the mid-1980s, when their Coliseum years were a distant memory, the Dodgers were routinely drawing three million fans a year to fifty-six-thousand-seat Dodger Stadium, completed in 1962 at a cost of $16 million.

Walter O'Malley, who predicted in the mid-1950s that the major league team that moved to Los Angeles would be the first to draw three million people per season, died in 1979, at seventy-two.

It was a boxing scene played out thousands of times before and since—an aging fighter, badly beaten, lies stretched out in a dark, dank locker room, while his handlers and a few newsmen inspect his battered, bleeding body. Only this time, it was a little different because Art Aragon was a little different.

They called him "The Golden Boy" because he could fill up Los Angeles's venerable old fight emporium, the Olympic Auditorium, like no one else in his time. But on this night, September 5, 1958, the Golden Boy was black, blue, bleeding—and at the end of the line. He'd just been horribly beaten by Carmen Basilio, a former world middleweight and welterweight champion.

Aragon began to groan, and clutched his abdomen. "Oh, I think I'm gonna be sick," he said. Then, looking up and seeing sportswriters surrounding him, he said: "Hey, any of you guys got a beer? I haven't had a beer in three weeks." That was The Golden Boy. In the end, he left 'em laughing. Colorful? Art Aragon invented colorful.

During the Basilio fight, after the point where the overmatched Aragon began to take a bad beating—early in the first round—Aragon's trainer, Lee Boren, begged him to be more aggressive with Basilio. Finally, between the sixth and seventh rounds, Boren said to him: "Art, if you don't start fighting this guy, I'm going to stop it."

Retorted Aragon, through his bloody mouth: "Why wait?" That was Arrogant Art, as he was also called, the fighter they loved to hate. Sometimes, Art would attend a card at the Olympic with a gorgeous blond and the booing would be so intense that the fight would have to be held up.

In the mid-1950s, he was the most recognizable sports figure in Los Angeles. In a sense, he was the king. Aragon had a way of getting into the news and staying there. The *Los Angeles Times* photo file on Aragon is nearly an inch thick. Pictures of Aragon fighting...out with beautiful women...in jailhouse fatigues...on his way to divorce court...Aragon arrested in another barroom brawl....

Columnists loved him. No one has ever filled a reporter's notebook faster or been quicker with a quotable quip. Of his $104,000 purse for the Basilio fight, the biggest of his career, he once said: "When I started fighting in 1944, I was broke. When I fought Basilio, they paid me $104,000 and I owed my ex-wives $200,000. What sense does that make?"

"Hey, in those days I owned this town," he told an interviewer in 1988. "It was just me and the Rams. Ask anyone who was around. Then those bleeping Dodgers moved to town, making page one every day and I had to start booking my fights around their games. I hate 'em. When I get up in the morning and see they've lost, it makes my whole day."

Aragon was back in the news in 1988. At sixty, he won a paternity suit. And with it, of course, a memorable Aragon quip. Seems Aragon's attorney had a doctor on the stand who told the judge: "Your honor, it is not possible for Mr. Aragon to have been the father of this woman's child."

Aragon jumped to his feet and said: "Your honor, I want a second opinion."

Then there's the story of his defeat by lightweight champion Jimmy Carter, a bout for which Aragon had to train down to 135 pounds. "I had a horrible time getting down to 135," Aragon said. "I was the first fighter in the history of the sport who had to be carried *into* the ring."

And of his last fight in 1960, when he lost to Alvaro Gutierrez, Aragon said: "My legs were so far gone I was useless. In the first round, I hit Gutierrez with my best shot, a right-hand right on the chin...and *I* went down."

For most of his career in Los Angeles (1944–60), Aragon was the fighter they loved to boo.

Aragon said the booing started in the late 1940s, on his way up, when he twice beat

In 1949 Art Aragon was still on his way up in boxing, the seventh-ranking lightweight, only five years after he entered the sport. Until his retirement in 1960 he was one of L.A.'s most successful and most colorful athletes.

Enrique Bolanos, a highly popular boxer from Los Angeles's Mexican-American community.

"He was an idol, I beat him bad, and they didn't like that," Aragon said. "But I started to notice that the more they hated me, the more they'd pay to see me fight."

By the late 1980s, after he'd turned sixty, Aragon was a successful bail bondsman in Van Nuys. He sat by the phone all day, waiting for calls from someone in jail, and sometimes reminiscing about his heyday with a guest. Displayed on his office walls were photographs of The Golden Boy, posing with Marilyn Monroe, Jayne Mansfield, and Mamie Van Doren.

"I didn't run with bums in those days, pal," he said. He points to an old, framed headline:

"Wife Sues Aragon, Names 15 Women"

"My first wife named fifteen women. My second wife divorced me and named nine women. My third wife divorced me and named two guys."

In 1988, an interviewer asked him what he missed from his boxing days.

"Nothin'!" he retorted. "I hated it! Boxing's a horrible sport. Getting whacked in the head, managers and promoters stealing my money, all that roadwork, tryin' to make weight....Whaddya mean, what do I miss?

"Well, OK, I do miss one thing.

"The broads."

Dodger manager Walter Alston and Yankee chief Casey Stengel introduce a huge Coliseum crowd on hand for a special exhibition game to honor popular Dodger catcher Roy Campanella, who had been paralyzed after an automobile crash following his team's last season in Brooklyn.

He sat there, in his wheelchair, at home plate, overwhelmed with one ovation after another sweeping down upon him from the vastness of the Los Angeles Memorial Coliseum. He cried a little, and so did many others in the crowd. And it was the crowd that was the story on this Thursday night, May 7, 1959. Attendance was 93,103, still the largest crowd ever to see a baseball game.

They'd come to honor onetime Dodger catcher Roy Campanella, the tragic, paralyzed victim of a 1958 auto accident. On this night, everyone paid to get in, even the Dodgers and their opponents, the New York Yankees.

In the mid-1950s, when the Dodgers played in Brooklyn, Campanella was one of sport's seemingly indestructible figures. He was one of baseball's best defensive catchers, a three-time National League Most Valuable Player award winner. "Campy" had hit 242 home runs in ten Dodger seasons and was one of baseball's most popular players. Then, tragedy.

It was raining hard on the night of January 28, 1958, when Campanella went into a skid on a highway a half-mile from his home in Glen Cove, New York. His car flipped over and crashed into a telephone pole.

Campanella's medical bills were enormous and would continue to grow for years. Before the start of the 1959 baseball season, the Dodgers and Yankees scheduled a rare in-season exhibition game at the Coliseum, with funds left over after the game earmarked for Campanella's medical care.

The Yankees had completed a series in Kansas City the previous night. They flew to L.A. at their own expense the following morning for the game, then flew the next morning to New York. The Dodgers played at San Francisco on the afternoon of the Campanella game, flew immediately afterward to L.A. for the Coliseum night game, then flew back to San Francisco after the game for the following night's game with the Giants.

And from all points in Southern California, people came not only to honor Campanella, but for a rare chance to see the New York Yankees. Rarely in Southern California history had there been a sports ticket as hot as this one.

The advance ticket sale for the game was eighty-two thousand, with ten thousand general admission seats at ninety and seventy-five cents set aside. Lines began forming at 2 P.M. Police that night estimated that fifteen thousand to twenty thousand outside the Coliseum didn't get in, although hundreds climbed over fences.

Thirty years later, Campanella could remember the exact attendance figure. "How could I forget?" he said, in a 1989 interview. "My gosh, all those wonderful people, 93,103 of them, who came out that night. You know, he never said so publicly, but Walter O'Malley took care of all my medical expenses. That man and the Dodgers were so wonderful to me. And as long as I live, I'll never forget that night."

In pregame ceremonies, when they wheeled the stricken "Campy" to home plate, it hurt to see him in the metal chair, his once-powerful hands twisted by paralysis. There were speeches, tributes, and ovation after ovation rocked the stadium.

When it came his time to speak, Campanella made it through without breaking. "I thank each and every one of you from the bottom of my heart," he said. "This is something I'll never forget as long as I live.

"I want to thank the Yankees for playing this game, and my old Dodger team, too. It's a wonderful tribute. I thank God I'm able to be here and see it."

Between the fifth and sixth innings came the most memorable moment of all. Campanella was wheeled to home plate again, and someone hit the light switches. The entire Coliseum was plunged into darkness, and on a signal, spectators lit matches and lighters. In the darkness, tiny flames flickered like millions of fireflies.

The Yankees beat the Dodgers that night, 6–2, but no one much cared. What mattered was that a stricken hero had felt, seen, and heard the love of 93,103 people.

# 1960 TO 1969

Cassius Clay clips ancient Archie Moore before a crowd of 16,200 fans at the Sports Arena in 1962.

**R**afer Johnson and C. K. Yang didn't know whether to laugh or cry at the Rome Olympics in 1960.¶ Although they represented different nations, they were close friends—UCLA teammates who'd shared hundreds of workouts, triumphs, and some heartbreak. They'd also shared the same dream for several years. Both wanted to win the decathlon gold medal at the Olympic Games.¶ Their story was similar to that of Jackie Fields and Joe Salas, the two Los Angeles Athletic Club boxers who wound up in the featherweight gold medal bout at the 1924 Olympics. In 1960, Johnson and Yang gave the Olympics and their coach, Elvin "Ducky" Drake, a decathlon to remember.¶ Rafer Johnson was the strapping son of a railroad section hand who raised a big family in the San Joaquin Valley farm town of Kingsburg, not far from Tulare, California, where another Olympic

decathlon champion, Bob Mathias, had grown up. Johnson was a multi-sport athlete at Kingsburg High School who was recruited by UCLA to play football.

"When I let UCLA know I was more interested in going to the Olympics than playing football I wound up with a track scholarship," he said years later.

Yang, whose real name is Yang Chuan-Kwang, is a member of the Takasago ethnic group, which inhabited the island of Taiwan centuries before the Chinese arrived. A natural athlete, Yang visited the United States as a teenager, trained briefly at UCLA, and met Johnson. At the time, Yang was already a well-known Asian athlete and he decided to enroll at UCLA. The China National Amateur Athletic Federation funded most of his stay at UCLA.

First, Yang spent a year and one summer in UCLA extension classes mastering English, then was accepted in 1958 as a fulltime student.

Johnson was an unusually big, strong athlete for the decathlon, 6′2″ tall and 205 pounds. Yang, leaner and faster but at 185 pounds not as powerful, had an edge in finesse and long running events. Johnson excelled in the hurdles and weight events.

In Rome, after the first day of the two-day event, Johnson was worried. He was in first place, with a 55-point lead. But what concerned him was that Yang was far closer to him than he'd been when they last competed.

The two finished one-two at the U.S. Olympic team trials at Eugene, Oregon, where Yang competed as a guest competitor. After the first day at Eugene, Johnson had a 195-point lead. In Rome, Yang actually bettered Johnson's marks in four out of five first-day events. But Johnson built a huge cushion in the shot put, beating Yang by nearly eight feet.

The first day was punishing for the entire field. Two thunderstorms interrupted the competition for a total of ninety minutes in the morning and evening. The first day's program wasn't completed until 11 P.M.

LEFT: Coach Elvin (Ducky) Drake helps to train one of his two decathlon superstars, C.K. Yang, who would compete for the Republic of China.

RIGHT: Rafer Johnson of Kingsburg, California won the Sullivan Award as the nation's top athlete of 1960, the year in which UCLA's former student body president won the Olympic decathlon.

Freshman C.K. Yang and graduate student Rafer Johnson work out together, aiming toward the Rome summer games.

Yang beat Johnson in a close 400 meters to finish the first day, 48.1 to Johnson's 48.3. The race was delayed over an hour after the second thunderstorm stopped because the starting blocks were underwater.

On the second day, which began at 9 A.M., the first event was a strong one for Johnson, the 110-meter high hurdles, where his lifetime best was 13.9. But he hit the first hurdle very hard and finished with a poor 15.3 while Yang ran 14.6. Johnson had lost the lead to his UCLA teammate.

Johnson was now in serious trouble, and he knew it. He had events coming up—the discus and javelin—where he was normally superior to Yang, but he knew he'd need more than a slim lead after nine events. The final event, the 1,500 meters, was a weak event for him.

"Competing against C. K. in those years meant I needed a big lead going into the 1,500 because he had a big edge on me there," he said.

Johnson regained a narrow lead in the discus, but Yang, who would later become a world-class pole vaulter, cleared 14′1¼″ and ordinarily would have overtaken Johnson at that point. However, Johnson, in a weak event for him, vaulted a lifetime best 13′5½″.

Now, even though Yang had cut Johnson's lead to 24 points, the pressure was on Yang. Only a very poor Johnson effort in the 1,500 meters would keep him from the gold medal. Yang also needed a big mark in the javelin, or a poor one by Johnson.

He lost on both counts. Johnson threw four feet farther than Yang in the javelin. So when they lined up for the 1,500, at 10 P.M., exhausted, Johnson had a 67-point lead. He needed only to stay close to secure the gold medal.

"Actually, I had an edge in that 1,500, even though C. K. was better than I was in the event," Johnson said years later.

"I knew that was my last race, so mentally that gave me an advantage. I knew it was my last decathlon. I can't remember if C. K. knew that or not, but at any rate I was prepared to do whatever it took to stay with him."

Johnson finished within six yards of Yang, running a lifetime best of 4:49.7. For Johnson, it was close enough. The two passed by the finish line, Yang first but knowing he hadn't won. The two UCLA athletes wobbled, nearly fell down from exhaustion, but finally collapsed into each other's arms.

Johnson showered and dressed and left the Olympic stadium at about midnight, alone. He walked the streets alone that night, an American in Rome, alone with his thoughts, alone with his victory.

"I walked around Rome all night, I didn't want to sleep," he said. "Near daybreak, an American student drove by, recognized me, and gave me a lift back to the Olympic Village."

In three Olympic Games, Rome proved to be C. K. Yang's only real shot at a gold medal. He'd finished eighth in Melbourne in 1956, and fifth in Tokyo in 1964. Johnson had finished second to winner Milt Campbell in 1956.

Today, Yang is the international competition director for Taiwan's Olympic Committee and does some coaching. He also owns a home in Thousand Oaks. He turned fifty-six in 1989.

Johnson, who was twenty-four in Rome, turned fifty-four in 1989. He never competed again. He lives in Sherman Oaks and is a consultant and national spokesman for Hershey's youth track and field program. He's also a consultant for Reebok Shoes. He was active in Senator Robert F. Kennedy's 1968 presidential campaign in California and was standing near Kennedy when he was assassinated, on the night of June 5, 1968.

On the evening of August 10, 1984, for about ten minutes, Rafer Johnson was the most visible human being in the world. Ten days before the opening ceremonies of the Los Angeles Olympic Games, Johnson was paged at a home for Jewish senior citizens in Canoga Park, where he had a speaking engagement.

On the phone was Peter Ueberroth, president of the Los Angeles Olympic Organizing Committee. Ueberroth asked if Johnson would visit him in his office following his speech.

"I didn't have a clue what he wanted," Johnson said later. "When I got there, Ueberroth asked me if I would run the last leg of the Olympic torch relay, and light the Coliseum torch.

"I was thrilled, and of course I told him I'd love to."

Thirty years after his victory in Rome, Rafer Johnson is probably best remembered for his long trip up the steep staircase to put the flame to the '84 Olympics.

Of that night in Rome, Johnson remembers the pain, as well as the elation. In the locker room late that night, Johnson talked to reporters while Yang sat on a stool nearby, crying. "I knew I had a working margin of about ten seconds [in the 1,500], but I wasn't going to let C. K. get away," he said that night. "We both held up. I wavered in the stretch, but so did he. I stuck to him like a buddy in combat."

The third place finisher, Vasily Kuznetsov of the Soviet Union, embraced Johnson and kissed him on both cheeks. Yang approached his old friend, shook his hand, and said simply, "Nice going, Rafe."

Johnson then indicated he was through with the decathlon. "I never want to go through that again—never," he said. "This is my last one, and you can print that." With that, Johnson walked out into the Rome night, saying: "I'm going out to look at the moon for a while."

A century or so from now, if some sports historian sits down and studies the twentieth century's boxing champions, his eye will be drawn to one historically significant match:

1962
*Nov. 15—Cassius Clay, Louisville, def. Archie Moore, San Diego; TKO 4, Los Angeles.*

Checking in the bio section of his old *Ring Record Book*, he'll see Moore at the time was something like forty-five years old, and that Clay, later to be known as Muhammad Ali, was twenty.

How in the world, he'll wonder, could one of the great heavyweight champions have wound up fighting Archie Moore at that stage of his career?

Possibly the historian will learn that in 1962 some folks were asking the same question in reverse. In other words, some wondered: "Isn't it a little soon for them to be throwing this kid in with a guy of Moore's experience?"

In the fall of 1962, Ali was 15–0 and thought to be a good heavyweight prospect. But no one then could know he would develop into the dominating champion of the late 1960s and early and mid-1970s.

Archie Moore, who would have 234 fights and an all-time record 145 knockouts in his career, had been fighting professionally for twenty-seven years the night he fought Clay. He'd been one of the great light-heavyweight champions and had fought twice—and lost—for the heavyweight championship.

There was a substantial number of boxing people that week who thought Clay, or the "Louisville Lip" as the mouthy Clay was called, would get his comeuppance against the veteran Moore.

One local ringsider, Dick Hathcock, watched Clay work out one day at the Main Street Gym, put on his disgusted face, and accosted *Los Angeles Times* sports columnist Sid Ziff.

"This Clay character has got nothin'," he barked at Ziff. "He wouldn't get this fight if it wasn't for you sportswriters building him up. He's strictly a product of your publicity. Fifteen fights, he's had! It's mismatches like this that helps kill off boxing. Moore's got punch, generalship, and experience going for him. What's Clay got? Nothin', that's what."

Early in the week of the fight, held in the Los Angeles Memorial Sports Arena, Las Vegas oddsmakers had posted Clay as an 11–5 favorite. On fight day, it was 3–1. But many saw it as a soft 3–1.

It should have been 300–1. In a fight that turned hot prospect Clay into a solid heavyweight contender, he left no doubts that he was now a force in the heavyweight division. He had knocked down the pathetically slow-footed Moore three times before referee Tommy Hart stopped it in the fourth round.

It was a bout that had drawn enormous curiosity, because it was the perfect boxing formula: young, hot heavyweight on the way up meets legendary opponent.

Despite record Los Angeles boxing ticket prices for the time—$7.50 cheap seats to $30 ringside—a crowd of 16,200 showed up. The gross gate, $182,599, was a California record.

Clay, in his first big payday, earned $35,000 from the live gate, then he and Moore earned about $15,000 each from theater closed circuit TV revenue. Moore made $65,000 from the live gate.

In an era when a major boxing show can earn tens of millions of dollars from home pay-per-view revenue alone, it's interesting to look back to Clay-Moore and note that the

promoter, Aileen Eaton, was "thrilled" at early reports that the fight had played to sellouts. Net profit on the theater telecast was about $200,000.

Almost before Moore's handlers had led their shaky fighter back to his corner, Clay rushed to the ropes and leered down at the formidable heavyweight champion, Sonny Liston, who glowered up at him from ringside.

"You're next!" Clay shouted at Liston. "And you will fall in eight!"

Barked Liston: "If you last eight seconds with me, I'll *give* you the title."

Fifteen months later, in Miami, Sonny Liston did exactly that. While seated on his stool after the seventh round, claiming a shoulder injury, he surrendered the heavyweight championship to Clay.

In the years ahead, after a two-year exile from boxing because he refused to be drafted into the Army during the Vietnam War, there would come Muhammad Ali's historic fights with Joe Frazier, Ken Norton, George Foreman, and Leon Spinks.

But on a pivotal night in Los Angeles in 1962, a young man knocked over an old man, and a legend was put in motion.

In northern San Diego County, on a dusty network of jeep trails that roll over 198 square miles of one of America's largest military bases, Camp Pendleton, lies the roots of one of America's great moments in the Olympic Games.

In the winter and spring of 1964, two U.S. Marine Corps lieutenants met at a jeep trail junction near their quarters in the DeLuz Housing Tract for officers and their families.

Beginning every Sunday morning, often at daybreak, they ran for hours. On some days, they followed a course that was thirty-four miles long.

One was a veteran marathon runner, Alex Breckenridge, who wanted to make the 1964 Olympic team. The other was Lieutenant Billy Mills, a twenty-six-year-old motor pool officer and a former University of Kansas runner. He wanted to run in the 10,000 meter race in Tokyo. Breckenridge didn't make it. Mills did, to understate the case.

The Mills story, a quarter-century later, still defies belief. On any list of America's greatest sports shockers, this one is still a solid number-one candidate.

The outline: half-Indian boy, orphaned at twelve, rises from wretched reservation poverty, has moderate success as a college distance runner, becomes discouraged, joins the Marines, makes the Olympic team—wins gold medal at the Olympics.

If it had never happened, and a screenwriter submitted it as a story, he'd be laughed out of Hollywood. But it happened. And they did make a movie out of his life. Billy Mills made it happen. Here's how:

In the spring of 1964, Camp Pendleton had an outstanding track team. There was Dave Davis, a sixty-foot shot putter in an era when sixty feet was a big deal; Ron Freeman, a great quarter-miler from Arizona State; and Dave Tork, a world-class pole vaulter.

Mills, a seven-sixteenths Oglala Sioux Indian who'd grown up on the Pine Ridge, South Dakota, reservation, was a miler and two-miler for Camp Pendleton in the spring of 1964, his best times, 4:11 and 9:03. More often than not, he didn't win in dual meets against the likes of San Diego State or Long Beach State.

In fact, six months before the Tokyo Olympics, Mills had never won much of anything. He'd only run in four 10,000-meter races, and in two of them failed to break a half-hour. After the Olympics, a reporter took a closer look at the Mills story and figured that he'd lost eighty

United States Marine Billy Mills, out of Camp Pendleton, stunned the running world by winning the 10,000 meters in the 1964 Tokyo Olympics over Tunisia's Mohammed Gammoudi (615) and Australia's Ron Clarke, among others.

percent of his races in the two years prior to the Olympic Games. At that point, his biggest track and field achievement had been a first place in the two-mile at the 1960 Big Eight Indoor Meet.

But Mills had a plan to become a winner. A BIG winner. The 10,000 meters, he figured, was perfect for him. And Breckenridge convinced him that months of marathonlike runs over Pendleton's hilly jeep trails would build up his body to the point where he could run with the world's best long-distance runners, then beat them with his exceptional finishing speed.

At the U.S. Olympic team trials at the Los Angeles Coliseum, few noticed when Mills made the team in the 10,000, finishing a distant second to Gerry Lindgren. Earlier that summer, Lindgren had upset two veteran runners from the Soviet Union in the Coliseum and was given a good chance for a gold medal at Tokyo.

Mills arrived in Tokyo in anonymity, a circumstance he felt was in his favor. "The fact that when I got to Tokyo no one knew who I was was an ideal situation for me," he said. "You know, when Lindgren sprained his ankle in a workout over there, I overheard an assistant coach say: 'It's a shame about Lindgren—all we have left in the ten is Mills.'"

The favorites in the race, after Lindgren was injured, were the tall Australian world record holder, Ron Clarke, Ethiopian Mamo Wolde, and Mohammed Gammoudi of Tunisia.

In addition to anonymity, Mills had two other things going for him in Tokyo—a strong finishing sprint and good health. For the first time in over a year, he had no injuries.

"In the spring and early summer of 1964, I had several injuries, including shin splints," he said. "Between May and September, I missed twenty-eight workout days. But it worked out that when I got to Tokyo, I was completely healthy.

"Also, three days before the race, I ran a 220 in 23.6 seconds. I knew then that if I could stay with Clarke and Gammoudi, I could beat them on the last lap. Really, people don't believe this, but I was confident I could win the race all along. I felt I had everything going for me. A month before the Olympics, I bought my wife a round-trip ticket to Tokyo."

Before the Games began, a *Track and Field News* panel of six experts handicapped every event. Not one picked Mills to finish even sixth.

On October 14, 1964, a capacity crowd of eighty thousand was in Tokyo's National Stadium for the opening day of track-and-field competition. Mills lined up with the crowded field, and waited for the starter's gun. No American, he knew, had ever finished higher than fifth in this race in the Olympic Games.

Throughout the race, Mills followed his strategy of running just behind the world-class runners in the race—Clarke, Wolde, and Gammoudi. Beginning at the midway point of the race, a large blister began to develop on his left foot. He ignored it.

With about two thousand meters left, Mills still found himself just behind Clarke and Gammoudi and ahead of Wolde, within striking distance of a huge Olympic upset. Wolde was beginning to labor.

Two other big-name runners, defending Olympic champion Pyotr Bolotnikov of the Soviet Union and Murray Halberg of New Zealand, had wilted under the fast pace and were well behind the leaders.

When they rang the bell for the last lap, Mills was lagging just behind Clarke and Gammoudi as they sped by a gaggle of runners who'd been lapped by the leaders.

On the first turn of the last lap, the crowd roared as the Tunisian army sergeant, Gammoudi, bumped Clarke, who inadvertently pushed Mills and sent him stumbling to the outside lanes. Mills recovered his balance, scrambled to make up the five yards he'd just lost, and got back in the race. As the huge crowd came to its feet in anticipation of a great finish, Mills charged down the backstretch, after Clarke and Gammoudi.

Gammoudi tried to steal the race again on the last curve, passing Clarke—and in the process bumping Mills again, with 150 meters to go.

It was an unforgettable sight—in a race where winners commonly win by margins of over one hundred meters, three runners were together in a mad dash for the tape. Mills came off the final turn and hit the throttle. With eighty meters to go, he sent the command to his body: "GO!" His sprint down the middle of the track carried him first past a shocked Clarke, who finished third, then Gammoudi.

It was over. He breasted the tape in a new Olympic record, 28:24.4. Seconds later, a Japanese judge rushed up to the exhausted Mills and asked: "Who are you?"

In the locker room, a reporter asked Clarke if he'd been worried about Mills.

"Worried about him?" the Aussie snapped. "I never heard of him!"

That morning, in Oceanside, California, near Camp Pendleton, news of Mills's victory came clattering over the wire in the newsroom of the *Oceanside Blade-Tribune*.

The city editor read the story, and walked by the author, then a youthful sportswriter.

"See who won the 10,000 in Tokyo?" he asked.

"No. Clarke?"

"No. Mills."

The youthful sportswriter nearly fell to the floor. He'd covered four Camp Pendleton dual track meets the previous spring, and not once had had reason to even mention Billy Mills's name. Mills? The gold medal? It wasn't possible—was it?

How big an upset? Late in 1964, in an Associated Press poll of sportswriters and broadcasters, Mills was given AP's Upset of the Year Award—over USC's 20–17 victory over Notre Dame and Cassius Clay's victory over Sonny Liston.

Twenty-five years later, the story reads as well as it did in 1964. Billy Mills is still the only American to have won the 10,000 meters in the Olympics. In fact, he's the only American to have finished higher than fifth since 1912.

Billy Mills, now a grandfather, turned fifty in 1989. He lives in Fair Oaks, California, where he owns an insurance business. On weekends, he jogs with his wife, Pat, on easy city park trails. He also gives motivational speeches, often to Indian groups.

Curiously, when he speaks on the subject of goal-setting and learning from defeat, he often cites the case of Ron Clarke, the heavy favorite he'd beaten in Tokyo.

"I asked him in Tokyo after the race what his plans were," Mills said. "I thought he might retire. He looked at me and said: 'I'm going to start all over, and the next time we race, you'd better be ready.'

"We raced five more times, never at 10,000, and he beat me every time. And do you know what he did after the Tokyo Olympics? He went to Europe and broke twelve world records in six weeks."

A quarter-century later, Mills said one of the best parts of his 1964 experience was the last part. Arriving home from Tokyo with Pat, late at night after the long drive from Los Angeles International Airport, he noticed the Camp Pendleton tract where he lived had a new entrance sign. He stopped the car, to read it with his high beams in the dim light:

DeLUZ HOUSING—HOME OF BILLY MILLS, OLYMPIC 10,000 METER CHAMPION

In a two-hour span on November 28, 1964, USC's football players fell precipitously from great heights of joy to tears of despair. And because they'd just participated in one of college football's great upsets, the pain went even deeper.

On that afternoon, before 83,840 at the Coliseum, the Trojans knocked unbeaten, top-ranked Notre Dame out of a certain national championship, 20–17.

During the locker room spray of soft drinks, cheering, and commotion of dragging fully clothed coaches into the showers and the general bedlam of young men celebrating a great victory, someone picked up a piece of chalk and wrote on the blackboard:

WE UPSET THE WORLD—BEAT MICHIGAN!

For a full hour, the victors celebrated. Then they slowly emerged from the locker room and departed for Enoch's Restaurant in South Gate, where a victory dinner party was to begin. When the crushing news came, some were just arriving at Enoch's, some were on their way, and some were still in the locker room.

The news was that faculty representatives of the Athletic Association of Western Universities had just voted to send Oregon State, not USC, to the Rose Bowl to play Michigan.

And so the party at Enoch's became a wake instead, one that lasted until 3 A.M.

The years have pretty much dulled the pain for those who played that day, but time will never fog over the joy of beating Notre Dame in November 1964.

They did it with 84-Z delay. That's a football play, not a car. USC, trailing 17–13, had taken the ball to Notre Dame's fifteen-yard line, where it faced a crucial fourth-and-8

Juan Marichal (27), then pitching for the Giants, took a swing at catcher John Roseboro for whizzing the ball back to Sandy Koufax too close to his head. The 1965 incident also involved Giant shortstop Tito Fuentes (26), coach Charlie Fox, Koufax, and both benches as umpire Shag Crawford tried to quiet things down.

situation. During a time-out, USC receiver Rod Sherman told Trojan coach John McKay he thought he could "get a step" on Notre Dame defensive back Tony Carey.

"Go ahead, take it to the huddle," McKay told him.

It worked. Quarterback Craig Fertig, who completed ten of fourteen passes in the second half, threw a crisp pass that Sherman caught at the three-yard line just as Carey climbed onto his back, and scored.

With the conversion, USC was ahead, 20–17, with 1:33 left. And that's how it ended. Notre Dame's season was suddenly over at 8–1 instead of the 9–0 everyone had expected, and USC was 7–3 instead of 6–4, as everyone expected. But more importantly, Oregon State was 8–2, and Rose Bowl–bound.

Mike Garrett, who became USC's first Heisman Trophy winner on that team, recalled the joy and the pain a quarter-century later. "Beating Notre Dame that day was one of the most exciting experiences of my life," he said. "I can't say it was more exciting than playing in two Super Bowls [with Kansas City], but it was a day I'll never forget.

"But at Enoch's that night, I walked in the door and I think it was Craig Fertig who came up to me and said: 'Guess what? They picked Oregon State.'

"I felt sick. I felt like I'd gone to a wedding that had been changed to a wake."

On a Sunday afternoon in San Francisco's Candlestick Park, on August 22, 1965, Los Angeles Dodgers catcher John Roseboro was hit by the pitcher, Juan Marichal.

Now, it's not like it sounds. Roseboro wasn't hit by Marichal's fastball or curve, or even his change-up. Marichal hit him with his *bat.*

The incident touched off a melee, and a riot was avoided only when cooler heads prevailed. Roseboro's head wasn't one of the cool ones. His was the one that was bleeding from a two-inch gash Marichal's bat had opened up.

The Marichal-Roseboro incident is probably still baseball's ugliest in the thirty-plus years major league baseball has been played on the West Coast.

Nobody sat this one out. Even if you didn't follow baseball, you had an opinion. Newspaper columnists couldn't wait to get to their typewriters. The Dodger-Giant rivalry grew hotter than ever. Marichal, who needed police protection afterward, received threats on the phone and in the mail. Roseboro sued him for $110,000.

It split the state in half, the northern part siding with Marichal and the Giants, the south with Roseboro and the Dodgers. National League president Warren Giles slapped Marichal with a $1,750 fine and when California Secretary of State Frank Jordan started a fund drive to help pay it, there was talk in the south of secession.

The Dodgers and Giants were in the heat of a pennant race when it happened. It was the third inning of a game the Dodgers were leading by 2–1. Marichal was at bat in the third, facing Sandy Koufax. Later, Marichal would claim that Roseboro's throws back to Koufax were being thrown just past the pitcher's ear and that the last one nicked him on the ear. Suddenly, a shocked, sellout crowd of 42,807 witnessed an incredible sight—Marichal, swinging his bat at Roseboro. Later, Roseboro said he barely managed to absorb some of the impact of the bat with his forearm.

In seconds both benches emptied, and fists flew. The Dodgers and Giants didn't much like each other anyway, but this went beyond rivalry. This was warfare. One of the prime peacemakers was Willie Mays, who pulled away some of his own teammates as well as some Dodgers.

The Giants hustled Marichal out of the stadium immediately afterward, while Roseboro went to the hospital for observation and stitches. By the time he left Candlestick, Dodger trainer Bill Buhler said Roseboro "had a knot on his head you couldn't cover with your hand."

Giles suspended Marichal for eight days as well as fining him. As for the $110,000 lawsuit, Roseboro settled for $7,500 in 1970.

Roseboro, who was fifty-six in 1989, is a minor league catching and pitching instructor for the Dodgers. Marichal lives in his native Dominican Republic and scouts Latin America for the Oakland Athletics.

It took nearly twenty years, but the two old rivals finally shook hands and closed the book on the incident at a Dodger Stadium old-timers game in 1982.

"We not only shook hands, but Juan invited my family and I to visit his family in Santo Domingo," Roseboro said. "We went down there for a vacation, had a nice time, and his daughters and my daughters became fast friends."

Double chin and all, retiring jockey Johnny Longden took George Royal to the post for the fifty-nine-year-old's last race, the San Juan Capistrano Handicap at Santa Anita.

Oh, the Giants won that 1965 game, 4–3. Or Willie Mays won it. First, Mays restored order. Then, moments later, he hit his thirty-eighth home run of the season, a three-run blast off Sandy Koufax that cleared the left-centerfield fence by forty feet.

Johnny Longden, one of racing's most successful jockeys, rode 6,032 winners over a forty-year career, and despite winning 452 stakes races—67 of them at Santa Anita—and 25 $100,000 races, it was No. 6,032 that folks remember the most.

Even the eyes of the most hard-bitten railbirds moisten over a bit when they remember March 12, 1966: The Last Ride of Johnny Longden.

By the mid-1960s, when he was in his late fifties, Johnny Longden wasn't getting the mounts, and therefore the respect, he used to. "Too old...he's lost it...ought to hang it up," were the whispers around the jocks' room, the paddock, and the grandstands.

Once, he was king. He rode Count Fleet to the Triple Crown in 1943. And he kicked the winner home in the unforgettable 1950 San Juan Capistrano Handicap, when Noor beat Citation by a nose.

In January 1966, Johnny Longden came down with a bad back—a gift from a fractious filly, Douceville. In the parade to the post, Douceville first threw Longden, then kicked him in the back just as he hit the turf. His orthopedist diagnosed it as a pinched nerve.

Recovery was slow, and it hastened his decision to retire and become a trainer. "Actually, it doesn't hurt when I ride, it only hurts when I walk," Longden told turf writers.

It worked out that The Last Ride of Johnny Longden, at age fifty-nine, would be aboard a Canadian horse, George Royal, at Santa Anita's $125,000 San Juan Capistrano Handicap, on Saturday, March 12, 1966.

The biggest crowd of the season, 60,792, turned out to watch the end of one of horse racing's great careers. There was no compelling reason to expect Longden would go out a winner. George Royal was a 7½-to-1 shot, and the old man wasn't the jockey he used to be— but let's go out and give the old guy a hand. You know, thanks for the memories. No, no one was fully prepared for The Last Ride of Johnny Longden.

Here's how *Los Angeles Times* turf writer Bion Abbott described it: "It couldn't happen this side of a movie studio, but it did. And there are 60,792 witnesses who can testify—if they have recovered their voices—that the old master, John Longden, captured the climactic closing race in his riding career with George Royal in the $125,000 San Juan Capistrano Handicap Saturday at Santa Anita.

"This turned out to be as thrilling a finale as any fiction writer could produce—only it was real. George Royal nipped Plaque by a nose at the end of the marathon mile and three-quarters in 2:48⅘. Probably the Old Pumper's forty years of riding experience made the winning difference during a spine-tingling, seesaw struggle through the stretch.

"During those dramatic twenty-five seconds of the final quarter, George Royal headed Plaque at the top of the stretch, lost his lead halfway home, and then came on again for Grandpa John in the final few steps to win with only a whisker to spare."

The big crowd cheered mightily when the announcer declared George Royal the winner after a photo review. And another great ovation began anew when Longden appeared in the winner's circle. Longden's wife, Hazel, and his daughter, Andrea, broke down and cried as the crowd's roaring tribute grew steadily in volume. Overnight, the very people who'd said Johnny Longden had lost it were saddened to realize his riding days really were over.

In 1989, at eighty-two, Longden had been training horses roughly half as many years as he'd ridden them. On that day in 1966, *Times* columnist Jim Murray seemed to sum up the racing world's feeling for Longden when he wrote: "A California race meeting without John Longden in the irons? Unthinkable! Insupportable! France without love. Paris without spring. Italy without music. Germany without bands. Baseball without beer. Weddings without tears."

Were it not for the involvement of history, no one today would have any reason to remember that the Green Bay Packers beat the Kansas City Chiefs, 35–10 in a routine game on the afternoon of January 15, 1967, at the Los Angeles Memorial Coliseum. As a game, this one wasn't much. These were Green Bay's great years under Vince Lombardi and they beat a lot of teams 35–10, or worse.

But this was a special football game. It was Super Bowl I, the first meeting of National Football League and American Football League teams following their 1966 merger.

The AFL, formed in 1960 by a group of millionaires that included Lamar Hunt and

ABOVE: Bart Starr passed his Green Bay Packers to victory over the Kansas City Chiefs at the Coliseum in Super Bowl I, the first meeting of the champions of the newly-linked American and National football leagues.

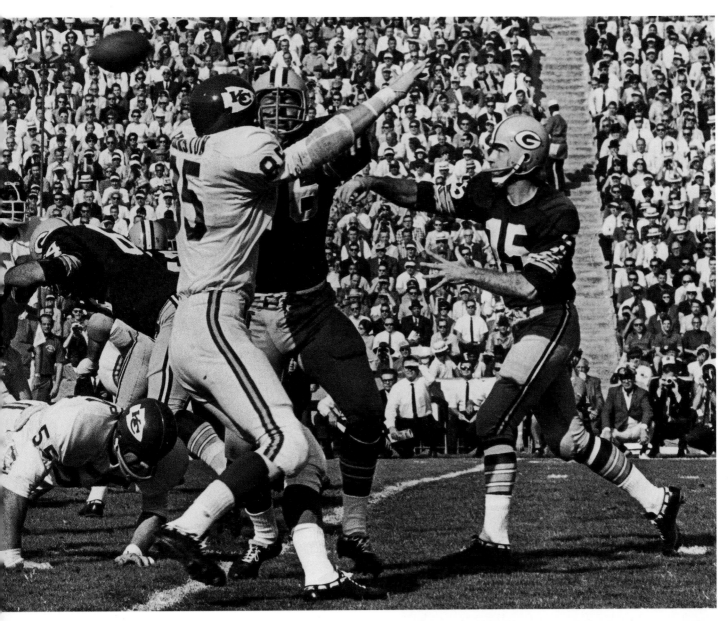

RIGHT: Famed Green Bay coach
Vince Lombardi barely broke a
sweat as his Packers dominated
Hank Stram's Chiefs.

Baron Hilton, spent millions in the early years keeping their young federation alive and credible. The size of the bonus checks the young league wrote out to college stars grew yearly as they paid fearful prices to stay even with the NFL in the talent wars. Finally, when the New York Jets in 1965 gave Alabama quarterback Joe Namath a bonus package totaling a then-astronomic $400,000, cooler heads from both sides stepped in and a merger plan was carved out.

NFL Commissioner Pete Rozelle announced in 1966 that the two leagues would play a January championship game in Los Angeles. Rozelle wanted the game to be known as "The World Championship Game." But he was quickly overruled by newsmen, who almost immediately dubbed it "Super Bowl," and Super Bowl it became.

Green Bay made it to Super Bowl I on New Year's Day by winning a last-minute thriller over Dallas, 34–27, while Kansas City beat Buffalo, 31–7. It set up a matchup of one coach, Vince Lombardi, who believed in simple offenses and defenses, executed to perfection, and another, Hank Stram, who favored multiple formations on both offense and defense.

In the two-week buildup to the Coliseum showdown, the Rozelle-ordered television blackout of the Los Angeles area generated almost as much newspaper copy as the game. Although there was widespread curiosity about the game nationwide, Rozelle believed the game was no cinch sellout in L.A., and he was right. For one thing, it was a heavy ticket—the house was scaled from $6 to $12. Even the price of the game program was a record—$1. Some felt the players' shares, $15,000 for the winners, $7,500 to the losers, was excessive.

Lawsuits were filed, politicians got into the act, and columnists ripped away at Rozelle when he refused to lift the blackout. Rozelle was simply exercising standard NFL policy, however. No NFL title game had ever been televised by a local station in the city where the game was played.

"Some of the writers objecting to the blackout," Rozelle said, "are the same writers who were telling me earlier that we had too much football on TV, that we were overexposing our product."

Meanwhile, Los Angeles football fans began securing hotel rooms in Santa Barbara, Bakersfield, and Las Vegas to watch the game.

As it turned out, Super Bowl I stands as the only one in the series that didn't sell out. But even though only 63,036 showed up, it was still the biggest grossing team sports event in history—about $800,000. And on a sunny, shirt-sleeve afternoon, before a surprisingly quiet, laid-back crowd, Green Bay took Kansas City to school and won with back-to-basics football. Although the Packers, thirteen-point favorites, led only 14–10 at halftime, they turned the game around on the third play of the second half.

On a third-and-five play from midfield, Kansas City quarterback Len Dawson tried to hit tight end Fred Arbanas on a short sideline pass. But Green Bay safety Willie Wood made a leaping interception at the Green Bay forty-five and returned it to the Kansas City five.

On the next play, Green Bay raised the lead to ten, then eleven points. As it turned out, the first NFL-AFL matchup was over.

In the Green Bay locker room afterward, Lombardi, from whom nary a negative word about the Chiefs could be prodded during the previous two weeks, said what everyone knew he'd say. Standing on a makeshift stage and staring into the glare of TV lights, he said: "I don't think that Kansas City compares with the top teams of the NFL. That's what you wanted me to say, and I said it."

Trailing Kenya's Kip Keino into the last lap of the 1,500 meters at the *Los Angeles Times* International Games at the Coliseum in July, 1967, Jim Ryun turned on the speed to win the race, establishing a record that stood for seven years.

In spite of his inability to win a gold medal in three Olympic Games, it may be that America never had a better middle distance runner than Jim Ryun.

Certainly no one ever looked the part better. He was a 6'2", 165-pound Kansan who ran with a long, graceful stride that also embodied power and great speed. The sight of Jim Ryun coming off the final curve of a race and kicking in his sprint was a sight that never left you. Here was a man born to run, and he was world class as a boy, before he was graduated from high school.

He was the first high school boy to break four minutes in the mile and he did it when he was a junior, at East High in Wichita. He competed in the 1964 Olympic Games at Tokyo while still a high school student. He had matured into his prime by 1968, and was thought of as the logical favorite in the 1,500 meters at the Mexico City Olympics. But he fell victim to the high altitude there, which favored Kenyans like Kip Keino, who beat him badly in the 1,500-meter final.

Surely, then, 1972 would be his year—but in a qualifying 1,500 heat at the Munich Olympics, his legs became entangled with another runner's and he fell, ending his Olympic career.

But between the 1964 and 1968 Olympics, no man had ever run like Jim Ryun.

On Saturday, July 8, 1967, 23,786 track fans at the Los Angeles Memorial Coliseum for the *Los Angeles Times* International Games saw him at his very best, the best he would ever be. He was matched in a widely anticipated 1,500 meters against Keino, expected then to be his chief rival at Mexico City.

Two weekends before the meet, Ryun had set a new world mile record, 3:51.1, at Bakersfield. The previous record was also his, 3:51.3.

When Ryun and Keino stood at the starting line, the world record for 1,500 meters was one of the track and field's most cherished marks. It was 3:35.6, set by Australian Herb Elliott at the Rome Olympics in 1960. It had withstood assaults of the world's best for seven years.

It seemed safe in this race, too, after a relatively slow 60.9-second first lap, with Keino slightly leading Ryun. Keino picked up the pace on the second lap, coming in at 1:57.2 at the 800-meter mark. Ryun, who said afterward his plan was to let Keino set the pace until the final lap, buried Keino and Elliott's record with 300 meters to go.

He passed Keino as if he were standing still, and steadily increased his lead in the back stretch. His long, powerful stride looked as if it could carry him clear back to Kansas. He sprinted to the tape 30 meters in front of Keino, in 3:33.1, setting a world record that would stand for seven years, until Filbert Bayi of Tanzania ran 3:32.16 in February 1974. Twenty-two years after Ryun's victory, only three Americans had run the 1,500 faster than Ryun did that day.

It was an overpowering performance. Keino, even though beaten by 30 meters, was clocked in at 3:37.2, at the time the ninth-fastest 1,500 ever. Statisticians say Ryun's 3:33.1 converts to a 3:50.2 mile.

Keino, a year later, would extract revenge in Mexico City, but on July 8, 1967, Jim Ryun had no way of knowing he would never be better, that this would be his finest hour.

"With 300 meters to go in that race, I felt absolutely great," Ryun said, years later. "I knew as soon as I started my sprint that I would win a fast race—I was never better than I was that day.

"And it really surprised me, because for the two weeks after the 3:51.1 mile I'd run at Bakersfield I'd been training at altitude at Alamosa, Colorado, in preparation for the Mexico City Olympics. I just couldn't run at altitude, I never could. When I got to L.A. I felt awful. I stayed at the USC dorms two days before the Coliseum meet—and slept all day long. I thought I'd run a terrible race that day."

Ryun was a spectator in the Coliseum the day of the 1,500-meter final at the 1984 Olympic Games. He was startled when it was announced that winner Sebastian Coe's time, 3:32.53, had broken his Coliseum record.

Ryun turned forty-two in 1989. He and his wife, Anne, live in Lawrence, Kansas. He travels around the country, running in masters 10,000-meter road races and making public-speaking appearances. When at home, he enjoys watching his children run. His daughter, Heather, was a letter winner on Kansas University's women's cross-country team in 1989, as a freshman. Twin sons Ned and Drew were both under two minutes in the half-mile as they entered their junior seasons at Lawrence High School. Daughter Catherine, at thirteen, looked like the first sprinter in the family, according to Ryun.

"We worried at first about them going into track, about how they'd take being compared to their father but they're great kids and it doesn't look as if it'll be a problem," Ryun said.

When you think about it, he shouldn't have worried. *No one* can be compared to Jim Ryun.

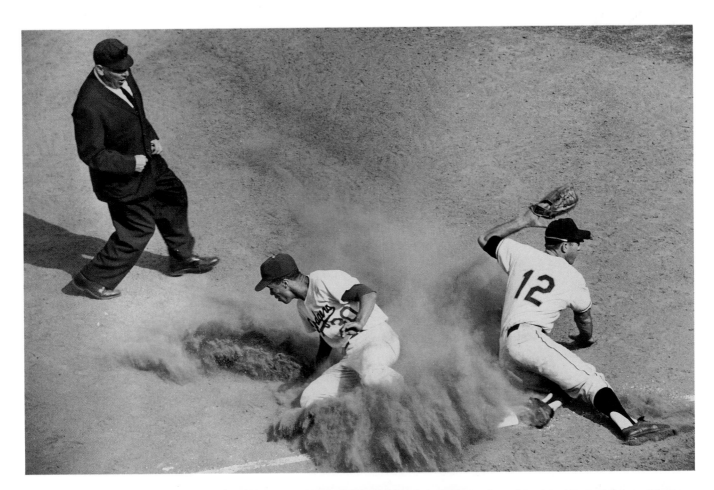

ABOVE: Maury Wills steals his 104th base as the ball eludes Giant third baseman Jim Davenport, enabling Wills to scamper home.

RIGHT: Low fives ruled the day as Sandy Koufax and John Roseboro celebrated the Dodgers' fourth straight win over the Yankees in the 1963 World Series; Koufax had also won Game Two.

LEFT: Dodger Stadium hosted a record crowd for the home opener against the Astros for the 1966 season.

RIGHT: A calm, eventempered Woody Hayes greets one of his Ohio State players as the Buckeyes fell to the UCLA Bruins in October, 1962.

ABOVE: "The Juice," O.J. Simpson, breaks away for a 64-yard touchdown run on November 18, 1967, as USC defeats UCLA 21–20 and earns a trip to the Rose Bowl.

FAR RIGHT: UCLA's giant star Lew Alcindor shows the press photographers that even a center knows how to dribble.

BY DWIGHT CHAPIN
Times Staff Writer

SAN DIEGO—John Wooden isn't
the sort of... basket-
basketball coach... his team's sh...
rs—after a... game.
So, in his... not as a college... fans
coach here... last night, his UCLA... not...
Bruins simply gave his 10th... play...
tional championship and going-a... Se...
resent, and... then walked off... dust...
oor after him—quietly, calmly, hap-
ly.
There was something special... Al...
owever, in the Bruins' 92-85 victory... ere...
er a rugged, stubborn Kentucky... and...
eam, something that comes along...
erhaps once... cecie... tha...
UCLA has... so many champion... eam...
ips that... of... em seem... uys...
most humo... all r...
But this o... was different or... It

# 1970 TO 1979

Champagne showers greeted Rick
Monday (16) and Bill Russell as L.A.
clinched the '78 pennant.

On the afternoon of September 6, 1970, a new, exciting era in automobile racing in Southern California seemed to have begun. A brand-new, $25.5 million auto racing plant, Ontario Motor Speedway, opened that day for the race many had already begun calling "Indianapolis West."¶ The huge, sprawling speedway complex was located forty miles east of downtown Los Angeles, just off the San Bernardino Freeway. The backdrop was pure postcard: the San Gabriel and San Bernardino mountain ranges appeared to be only a few blocks away.¶ The first race was called the "California 500," and the promoters of the speedway's first major race weren't at all embarrassed at emulating the Memorial Day classic at the Indianapolis Motor Speedway. They even hired the Indy track's president, Tony Hulman, to

Ontario Motor Speedway, home of the California 500, gave Southern California its duplicate of Indy, but ten years after its 1970 opening it was demolished.

begin the race by yelling into the microphone his famous cry: "Gentlemen, start your engines!"

On cue, engines roared. So did 180,223 spectators. It's still believed to be the largest crowd ever to see a sporting event in Southern California. And what they saw that sunny, windy Sunday afternoon turned out to be an auto racing classic.

Jim McElreath, a forty-two-year-old Texan who started in the sixth row, won the 500-miler by two seconds in a finish that was nearly beyond belief, even to veteran auto race enthusiasts. First, it was a punishing race, in which only seven of thirty-three starters finished. Second, it was an epic finish, with the lead changing hands five times in the last twenty miles, and twice on the next-to-last lap.

McElreath, in a Ford turbocharged Coyote owned by A. J. Foyt, took the lead on the front straightaway on the 196th lap, twelve and a half miles from the finish. But he lost the lead to runner-up Art Pollard in a thrilling, seesaw stretch run.

McElreath recaptured the lead on turn four of lap 198 and had about thirty yards on Pollard when he crossed the finish line to win first-place money of $146,850.

Seldom anywhere had an auto race taken such a toll on machines. Some of racing's biggest names had been left by the wayside by the time McElreath and Pollard were waging their stretch duel. Al Unser, Mario Andretti, A. J. Foyt, Dan Gurney, George Follmer, LeeRoy Yarbrough, Joe Leonard, and Peter Revson all failed to finish.

For most of the race, Unser looked like the runaway winner. He led for 166 laps. At one point, with thirty-five miles to go, he had three-and-a-half miles on runner-up Revson. But with 14 laps left, his turbocharger blew up.

And so for one afternoon, a mob of Southern Californians shared the same kind of excitement as the ten-thousand-odd who showed up at Los Angeles's Agricultural Park on

Motor racing of a different sort fills the streets of Long Beach during trials for a Grand Prix race there in 1978.

that November afternoon in 1903, when Barney Oldfield came to town and thrilled spectators with his mad, dust-raising dashes around a horse racing track.

And now, surely, the California 500 and the Ontario Motor Speedway meant that Southern California had finally reclaimed its lost title as America's auto racing capital. Surely, the California 500 would give the Indy 500 a run for its fame and notoriety.

Sadly, it would never be. On December 16, 1980, the 680-acre facility, which never turned a profit for its owners, was sold to developers for $35 million. On July 23, 1981, wrecking crews arrived and installed a giant rock crusher in the infield. There, the facility's two-and-a-half-mile asphalt track and its concrete structures were smashed up into pebbles. The speedway's 140,000 aluminum seats, which required twenty-three miles of aluminum tubing to construct, were ripped out and sold to other speedways.

Today, there is a shopping center on part of the old speedway grounds. But most of the site is still vacant land. Tumbleweeds blow over barren ground where the finish line once was, where in but a twinkling of time, tens of thousands cheered Jim McElreath's memorable stretch run in the first California 500.

Years ago, when asked how one coach, John Wooden, could possibly win ten NCAA basketball championships, Marquette University coach Al McGuire suggested that Wooden won with simplicity.

"Wooden's success was due to more than the fact that he had great athletes," he said. "Other schools had great athletes, too. But he won all the time, and they didn't. He won because he took great athletes, gave them very simple patterns and plays, and made them repeat them over and over until they did it to perfection."

There is a body of opinion in sports, one that grows in size as the years go by, that John Wooden was the greatest coach in U.S. sports history, in any sport.

Between 1964 and 1975, Wooden won an astounding ten NCAA championships. By 1989, more than a decade after Wooden had retired, no other coach had won more than three. Equally remarkable was that Wooden's teams were at their best in prime time, in championship games. Most commonly, if you met UCLA in the NCAA title game, you got hammered. Of his ten national championship teams, his second-closest game in the NCAA championship game was a six-point win over Villanova, in 1971.

And it is that team, the 1971 Bruins, that many point to as the proof of Wooden's greatness as a coach.

"Looking back on all his championship teams, that was the one year where you could say Wooden wasn't necessarily the favorite to win it all," said Bob Boyd, who coached USC during the Wooden reign. "I didn't feel then that that team was necessarily the best one in the country. That team had four starters who made it in the NBA, but it didn't have the dominating player, like an Alcindor or a Walton."

The '71 Bruins fell between UCLA dynasties, the Lew Alcindor–led teams that won three 1960s championships—and put together an eighty-eight-game win streak—and the Bill Walton–led teams of the early 1970s that won two titles.

In 1971, Wooden had an experienced team returning, featuring the agile, aggressive front line of Sidney Wicks, Steve Patterson, and Curtis Rowe. The backcourt starters were long-range shooter Henry Bibby and a superb defensive guard, long-armed Kenny Booker.

Those players had won the NCAA crown the year before, and returned for the 1970–71 season having lost to graduation a dominating guard, John Vallely. It was more than a good team, it was an outstanding team of good athletes whom everyone expected to play well together. But not many sized it up as a dominating team, nor as a team that was a cinch to make the Final Four, let alone win another national title.

In the western regional finals at Salt Lake City, it looked as if UCLA had played out its string. Down 31–27 to Cal State Long Beach at halftime and by 44–33 with fourteen minutes left, UCLA called on all its resources to pull out a 57–55 victory. Once again, UCLA was on its way to the Final Four, this time at Houston's Astrodome.

The Bruins beat Kansas in the semifinals, 68–60, and went to the title game against Villanova, a 92–89 double-overtime winner over Western Kentucky.

It was Saturday afternoon, March 27, 1971. Before 31,765, the Bruins' crown trembled

Following in the footsteps of Lew Alcindor, UCLA's Bill Walton takes it to the hoop for Coach John Wooden in 1973.

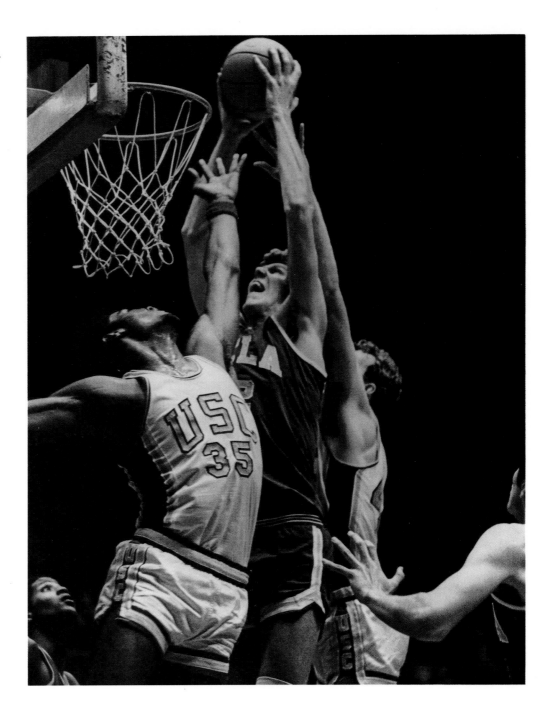

and wobbled, but it did not fall. In the end, the old Wooden trademarks all fell into play—coolness, poise, and patience—and UCLA won its fifth straight NCAA title and its twenty-eighth straight NCAA tournament game.

In the first half, Bibby connected on long bombs he launched over Villanova's zone defense and Patterson scored twenty inside. UCLA ran off to a 45–37 halftime lead. Then Wooden surprised everyone by opening the second half with a stall, and brought Villanova out of its zone.

The strategy nearly backfired, because the Wildcats suddenly caught fire coming out of their zone. With 5:09 left, Villanova had cut the lead to 58–54 and again to 61–58 with 2:38 to go.

But in the stretch, UCLA calmly dealt with the challenge. From 63–60, Bibby coolly sank three free throws, and Patterson made a lay-up.

Afterward, Villanova coach Jack Kraft echoed a familiar theme. "They win because they're so tremendously well drilled," he said. "They don't try to do anything but the basics. They run their pattern at you, and if it doesn't work they do it again and again and keep doing it until it does work.

"I could see it today—they executed and did things a little smoother than we did."

After 1971, with the first of the Bill Walton teams suiting up for the following season, UCLA went on to win three more NCAA championships, and stretched its amazing NCAA tournament win streak to thirty-eight games. It was snapped in 1974 by North Carolina State, 80–77, in a double-overtime NCAA semifinal game.

The following year, however, Wooden won his tenth national championship by beating Kentucky in the 1975 championship game. Then at 64 he retired.

In 1989, Wooden was asked what would please him most fifty years later, when people reflected on his UCLA teams.

"I think I'd be happiest," he said, "if they realized we won tall, short, and with inexperience. My first championship team [1964] didn't have a player over 6′4″. My 1967 team was almost all sophomores. My 1970 team was practically an all-new team, and we went from the low-post offense we'd used for three years with Lew Alcindor to a high-post with Steve Patterson, and it worked."

Asked about McGuire's analysis of his coaching technique, he paused a while, and said: "Well, basketball is not a complicated game. And I think a lot of coaches today try to make it complicated."

UCLA in NCAA championship games:
1964—UCLA 98, Duke 83
1965—UCLA 91, Michigan 80
1967—UCLA 79, Dayton 64
1968—UCLA 78, North Carolina 55
1969—UCLA 92, Purdue 72
1970—UCLA 80, Jacksonville 69
1971—UCLA 68, Villanova 62
1972—UCLA 81, Florida State 76
1973—UCLA 87, Memphis State 66
1975—UCLA 92, Kentucky 85

Early on the morning of January 11, 1972, the coach of the Los Angeles Lakers, Bill Sharman, was up early, prowling the lobby of the Pfister Hotel in Milwaukee.

Sharman didn't sleep much anyway on Laker road trips and on this night he hadn't slept at all. The Lakers had been beaten by the Bucks the previous afternoon, 120–104. The longest winning streak in the history of professional team sports, thirty-three consecutive victories, was over.

Sharman was startled, then, to see *Los Angeles Times* sportswriter Mal Florence, bags packed, at the front desk. He was checking out. Strange, Sharman thought. There were still two games left on the Lakers' road trip.

This was in the days when metropolitan newspaper sports departments didn't automatically cover every NBA road game. But in L.A., the Laker win streak had been big news.

Florence had a brief message from the office waiting when he returned to his hotel the previous day, after the Lakers had lost: "Come home."

Striding to the front desk, Sharman said: "Hey, Mal—you're leaving?"

"Sorry, Bill," Florence said. "We don't cover losers."

With that, Florence walked out of the lobby, climbed into a cab, and left, leaving behind an open-mouthed Bill Sharman.

The 1971–72 Lakers, the NBA champions, were one of the NBA's dominant teams. They were anchored deep in the post by 7′1″ tall, 265-pound Wilt Chamberlain, then thirty-four but still a force in his sport. He was no longer a fifty-point-per-game scorer, as he'd been a decade earlier. But on rebound plays, when the ball was up for grabs and elbows and forearms flew, he could be frightening.

"One time Wilt hit me on the top of my head with an elbow, and when I turned to run up the court, I wasn't sure I was running in the right direction," said Dennis Awtrey of the Philadelphia 76ers.

The team's leading scorers were guards Jerry West and Gail Goodrich, and flanking Wilt on the front line were forwards Happy Hairston and Jim McMillian. The primary subs were guards Flynn Robinson and Pat Riley and Wilt's relief man, Leroy Ellis.

How good were they? How about unbeaten for two months? From November 5, 1971, to January 9, 1972, they were 33–0. No other NBA team has ever approached that winning streak, nor has any team in a major sport. In fact, the only NBA team ever to win twenty straight was the Bucks, who'd done it the previous season.

By 1989, Pat Riley, who'd been the number-three substitute for the 1971–72 Lakers, had coached the Lakers to three NBA championships in the 1980s. He was asked how the thirty-three-in-a-row team compared to the championship Laker teams of the 1980s.

"Based on what that '71–'72 team accomplished, there's no doubt in my mind it was the greatest one-year team ever," he said. "I mean, they won thirty-three in a row and walked through the play-offs. If that team played the Lakers' 1985 team, it would've been a good game, but I'd still pick the 1972 team."

But it came to an end on a Sunday afternoon in Milwaukee against the defending NBA champion Bucks in a nationally televised game. The Lakers' twenty-four turnovers and thirty-nine percent shooting, combined with Milwaukee center Kareem Abdul-Jabbar's thirty-nine points, twenty rebounds, and short right hand, brought about the inevitable.

In the second quarter, Abdul-Jabbar, incensed at a perceived Hairston foul, caught Hairston on the jaw with a short right-hand punch that put the Laker forward on the deck for about a six-count. Afterward, the Lakers complained meekly that Abdul-Jabbar should've been ejected.

In the streak, seventeen wins were at home, sixteen on the road. Eight times, the opponent was held to fewer than one hundred points. In one game, the Lakers' defense held Buffalo to ten points in one quarter. When it ended, they'd had two perfect months—and no one else has ever had *one.*

For snapping their streak, the Lakers got even in the play-offs. Sharman's team beat Milwaukee, four games to two, in the Western Conference play-offs then captured the NBA crown by flattening the New York Knicks, four games to one.

On January 1, 1973, USC's football team was confronted with an opportunity not often presented to college football teams: by winning one football game, the Trojans could win the national championship. They decided not only to do that, to beat Ohio State in the Rose Bowl, but also to put an exclamation mark at the end of their season. A perfect season, 12–0.

Some college football scholars point to John McKay's 1972 Trojans as not only USC's best-ever football team, but perhaps one of the great teams of college football's modern era. The criteria are plentiful:

—USC's closest game that season was a 30–21 win over Stanford.

—The team scored more than fifty points in three games, more than forty in seven.

—In seven games, the Trojans allowed one touchdown or fewer. In four consecutive conference games, they allowed a total of two touchdowns.

—Finally, in the Rose Bowl, if there were any doubts left, USC hammered a very good Ohio State team, 42–17.

The '72 Trojans comprised a remarkable pool of talented athletes, and some were cut from rare molds.

Take Pete Adams, for instance, and his crazy dog, Turd. Adams, an offensive tackle, was the team's nonconformist. He showed up for practice every day in sunglasses, battered Hawaiian shirt, shorts, and sandals...and with Turd.

Turd, until Adams adopted him, was a street dog. He never knew his parents. Turd had one great joy in life—wind sprints on the USC football practice field. Turd ran 'em all. The more punishing the wind sprints, the more Turd liked them, running alongside the players, nipping at their heels.

Pete Adams and five teammates, according to one of the team's quarterbacks, Pat Haden, were the best part of the '72 Trojans.

Haden, by the late 1980s, was working for a Los Angeles law firm, stationed behind an eight-foot-wide desk. "I was a sophomore that year, behind Mike Rae, and played a little bit," he said. "When I handed the ball off on running plays, it was common for me to turn around and see the ballcarrier going through a hole as wide as this desk."

Sophomore Anthony Davis stuns 78,243 Coliseum fans and the Notre Dame kickoff team, and delights his bench with a 97-yard touchdown, the first of six, in a 45–23 USC victory.

The primary offensive tackles that year were Booker Brown, Adams, and Steve Riley. Center Dave Brown and guard Mike Ryan were among the best in college football. And Charles Young was an all-world blocker at tight end.

"It was an interesting mix of guys," Haden said. "Adams was the team character, Mr. Nonconformist. Mike Ryan was a straight-arrow, religious type. Yet they played side by side all year, and complemented each other very well."

Viewed years later, USC's 1972 roster carries more clout than it did in 1972. A split end/acrobat named Lynn Swann wound up in the NFL Hall of Fame. Anthony Davis, who on one afternoon in 1972 scored six touchdowns against Notre Dame, was a relatively unheralded, second-string tailback when the season began. Young, Sam Cunningham and Adams were all first-round NFL draftees. Swann was a first-rounder the following year, and another wide receiver, Edesel Garrison, was also a high NFL pick.

Some of the defensive standouts were linebacker Richard Wood—still USC's only three-time All-American—tackle Jeff Winans, and ends John Grant and Karl Lorch.

The starting quarterback, Mike Rae, remembers the team as a mature one, talented, and one with luck on its side. "What you had with that team was a big group of very good, experienced athletes, all of whom became seniors at the same time and all of whom had relatively injury-free seasons," he said.

It all came down to January 1, 1973, on a day when the principal cast of characters would be a fullback named Sam, a coach named Woody, and a photographer named Art.

About two hours before the game, when virtually no spectators were in the Rose Bowl, *Los Angeles Times* photographer Art Rogers approached the prickly Ohio State coach, Woody Hayes, for a close-up. Seeing Rogers approaching with his camera, Hayes charged. Hayes, Rogers said later, jammed the camera into his face.

Rogers, with cuts on his face, left the Rose Bowl for emergency-room treatment at a Pasadena Hospital. Few had seen the incident, and by game time hardly anyone in the stadium knew it had happened.

Meanwhile, the two teams played sluggishly in the first half, to a 7–7 intermission tie.

But in the second half, USC's potent ground game erupted. The Trojans scored the first five times they had the ball, and turned the game into a rout. Fullback Sam Cunningham scored five times with end zone dives over the line of scrimmage.

In the locker room, McKay was matter-of-fact about what his team had just demonstrated. "We won, so we must have better players," he said.

Just before the game, *Los Angeles Times* reporter Mal Florence had received a call from the *Times* sports desk, informing him of Rogers's run-in with Hayes. Don't fail to get Hayes's version, he was told.

"Woody was polite during the postgame interview session, but I knew my question would be the last one, so I waited," Florence recalled.

Finally: "Coach, Mal Florence, *Los Angeles Times*. Could you comment on your assault on *Los Angeles Times* photographer Art Rogers before the game?"

Hayes's face twisted into a dark storm cloud. His eyes bulged as he shouted: "Why you dirty [...] he wasn't hurt!"

Two days later, Rogers filed battery charges against Hayes.

Three months later, Rogers dropped the charges, explaining he'd received "an appropriate communication" from Hayes.

In 1989, Haden was asked what his most vivid memory was of the 1973 Rose Bowl game. "I remember being run out of bounds at the Ohio State bench, near where Woody was throwing a temper tantrum at either the officials or his players," he said.

"He took off his glasses, threw them on the ground and stomped on them. But almost in the same motion, his trainer handed him another pair."

A couple of days after the Rose Bowl game, Hayes paid USC the ultimate tribute. The Trojans, he said, were "the best college team I've ever seen."

Woody Hayes died in 1984. Art Rogers, considered one of America's best sports photographers, retired in 1983, after forty-six years at the *Los Angeles Times*, and lives in Morro Bay, California, where he fishes "as often as I can." Pat Haden is a venture capitalist and a TV football commentator, Mike Rae is a PE instructor at Orange Coast College, and Pete Adams lives in Leucadia.

Turd, sad to report, died in 1982.


If it wasn't the most exciting college football game ever played in the Coliseum, it certainly makes the top three.

USC, once trailing 24–0, scored fifty-five unanswered points, forty-nine of them in the second half, for a 55–24 victory over Notre Dame. Yes, that's not a typo. *Notre Dame.* USC coach John McKay summed it up best by saying: "I still don't know what happened. I can't understand it. Maybe against Kent State—but Notre Dame?"

Seldom has a college football team been aflame as were the USC Trojans on the afternoon of November 30, 1974. And the athlete wielding the match, the man who snapped his teammates out of the doldrums, was a 5′9″ tall, 185-pound comet named Anthony Davis.

Notre Dame, coming into the game with a 9–1 record, was the top-ranked defensive team in America. USC was 8–1—and a four-point favorite.

If you saw this one, you saw two games. Notre Dame almost routinely rolled over the Trojans in the first half, outgaining USC 257 yards to 143, and piling up a first down edge of 18–7. At intermission it was 24–6.

Davis, who would score four touchdowns on the day, scored the first one with ten seconds left in the first half on a 7-yard pass from Pat Haden. Then, on the second-half kickoff, he brought 83,552 people to their feet with an electrifying 102-yard return.

That play lit the Trojans' fuse.

After that, USC partisans scarcely found time to stop cheering and sit down in the third quarter. When the quarter ended, USC had a 41–24 lead. In fact, the Trojans went from 6–24 to the lead, 27–24, in nine minutes, thirty seconds of playing time. It was even too much for the Coliseum scoreboard, which went on the blink in the third quarter.

When the fire was put out, USC had registered a 49–0 second half. With eight minutes to play in the game, McKay began pulling his starters and sending in the subs.

Some highlights:

—John McKay, the coach's son, caught four passes for 110 yards and two touchdowns in the third quarter.

—Haden completed his first six passes in the quarter for 139 yards and three touchdowns.

—Davis's kickoff return was his sixth and set an NCAA career record. Also, his four touchdowns were his forty-ninth, fiftieth, fifty-first, and fifty-second at USC.

Davis was asked for an explanation as to what had happened to his team in the second half, and his explanation made as much sense as anyone's.

"We turned into madmen," he said.

Since 1953, the Dodgers have had two field managers. Walt Alston, who took over for Charley Dressen in 1953, was the team's last manager in Brooklyn, ran the team in its Coliseum years in Los Angeles, and then managed the team for fifteen seasons in Dodger Stadium. After twenty-three seasons, he retired in 1976 and was replaced by a man bearing similar traits of loyalty to the Dodger organization, Tommy Lasorda.

Alston died in 1984. The day after he died, Dodger radio man Vin Scully came up with the best one-sentence character sketch of Walt Alston, the quiet man: "I always imagined him as the type who would ride shotgun on a stagecoach through Indian country," Scully said.

That was Walt Alston—strong, silent, but in command.

In many ways, Lasorda was the opposite. Lasorda likes to talk. And one of his favorite themes is Dodger loyalty.

Lasorda was once a left-handed pitcher in the Brooklyn Dodger organization. When his playing days were over, in 1961, the club offered him a $6,000-per-year scouting job and he happily took it.

Lasorda's dream was to one day manage the Dodgers. He waited sixteen years, and they were long, hard years of low-salaried minor league jobs before he became Alston's third-base coach in 1973.

From his East Coast scouting job, Lasorda was promoted in 1965 to a Rookie League managing job, which meant a $500 raise, up to $7,000. He performed well, and was promoted all the way up to triple-A. His salary skyrocketed to $9,000.

After four years of managing the Albuquerque Dukes, Lasorda was summoned to Los Angeles, as Alston's third-base coach. Starting salary: $15,000.

"Those were tough years for Tommy. He was raising two kids and he and Jo [his wife] lived in a small, two-bedroom apartment," remembered an old friend. "He used to come early to Dodger Stadium, so he could use the club's laundry room to do the family laundry."

Lasorda's faith that his loyalty would be rewarded never wavered. Twice, as the third-

Parking spaces were at a premium at Dodger Stadium on October 4, 1977 for the first game of the National League playoffs against the Philadelphia Phillies.

base coach and without any guarantee he would succeed Alston, he turned down managing offers from two teams. "I was gambling," he said. "I was betting that my loyalty and dedication and contributions would one day be rewarded."

Tommy Lasorda's reward came on September 29, 1976.

Dodger President Peter O'Malley had called Lasorda at home late the previous evening and told him: "I want you to be by your phone early tomorrow morning." Recalled Lasorda, in 1989: "I think I slept in the chair, by the phone, all night."

Answering the call on the first ring early the next morning, Lasorda heard O'Malley say: "Come on in; we're going to hold a press conference and we'll announce you as the manager of the Los Angeles Dodgers."

By 1989, after six trips to the playoffs, four National League pennants, and two World Series championships, Lasorda's Dodger salary was about $500,000, a sum exceeded by his endorsements income.

That's Tommy Lasorda, the ultimate company man—a guy who started with his firm at $6,000 per year and rose to $500,000 per year.

As Don King likes to say, only in America.

And in 1976, when he replaced Alston, Lasorda revealed something about his priorities, the value he placed on loyalty. Of Alston's twenty-three years, Lasorda said: "It's a great achievement, managing the same team for twenty-three years. I compare this with getting three thousand hits or three hundred pitching victories."

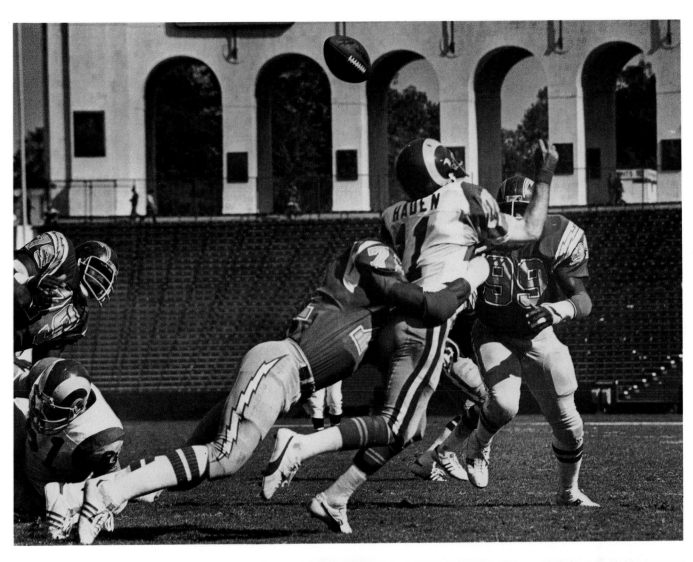

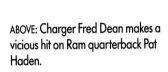

ABOVE: Charger Fred Dean makes a vicious hit on Ram quarterback Pat Haden.

RIGHT: Before he traded the sidelines for the press box, John Madden led the Oakland Raiders over the Minnesota Vikings 32–14 in Super Bowl XI at the Rose Bowl in Pasadena.

ABOVE: Inglewood Forum fight fans watched Ken Norton tag former champion Muhammad Ali with a solid left in their 1973 rematch, but Ali prevailed with a furious 12th-round rally to win the split decision.

LEFT: *Times* photographer Ken Hively captures a pensive champion.

OPPOSITE PAGE: Tennis in the Southland saw all the great champions come to play in the 1970s: the Chris and Jimmy show made headlines on sports pages as well as in gossip columns; local girl Rosie Casals's effervescent play made friends everywhere.

# 1980
## TO
# 1989

Magic Tells
the
Let

By TED GREEN
Times Staff Writer

PHILADELPHIA — The season
started with Magic Johnson gleefully
hugging Kareem Abdul-Jabbar after
the captain tossed in a skyhook at the
final buzzer to win the opener in San
Diego.

Six months later, the season ended
with Magic Johnson gleefully hugging the National Basketball Assn.'s
championship trophy.

"I know your ankle hurts,
Kareem," Johnson said, "but why
don't you get up and dance, anyway?"

All the champagne-popping late
Friday night, bottles of champagne

THE MAGIC NUMBERS

LOS ANGELES

| | Min | FG | FT | R | A | P | T |
|---|---|---|---|---|---|---|---|
| Chones | | 9 | 1-1 | 10 | 3 | 2 | 11 |
| Wilkes | 42 | 16-30 | 5-5 | 10 | 4 | 3 | 37 |
| Johnson | 47 | 14-23 | 14-14 | 15 | 7 | 3 | 42 |
| Nixon | 40 | 1-10 | 2-2 | 3 | 9 | 3 | 4 |
| Cooper | 39 | 4-9 | 8-9 | 4 | 6 | 4 | 16 |
| Lndsbrgr | 19 | 2-7 | 1-2 | 10 | 0 | 4 | 5 |
| Holland | 9 | 3-4 | 2-2 | 0 | 0 | 2 | 8 |
| Byrnes | 1 | 0-0 | 0-0 | 0 | 0 | 0 | 0 |
| Totals | 240 | 65-92 | 33-35 | 52 | 27 | 22 | 123 |

Shooting: Field goals, 60.7%; free throws, 91.4%.

PHILADELPHIA

| | Min | FG | FT | R | A | P | T |
|---|---|---|---|---|---|---|---|
| Erving | 29 | 13-23 | 1-4 | 7 | 3 | 4 | 27 |
| C Jones | 26 | 2-3 | 2-2 | 6 | 2 | 4 | 6 |
| Dawkins | 31 | 6-9 | 2-5 | 4 | 1 | 5 | 14 |
| Hollins | 26 | 5-13 | 3-4 | 1 | 6 | 4 | 13 |
| Cheeks | 40 | 5-11 | 3-3 | 2 | 8 | 2 | 13 |
| B Jones | 29 | 4-8 | 0-0 | 9 | 1 | 4 | 8 |

Laker domination of NBA basketball in the 80s, including back-to-
back championships, came to a
thrilling halt in the 1989 finals,
when Byron Scott and his teammates couldn't stop Isaiah Thomas
and his Detroit Piston teammates
from taking the title.

Of all the Southern California superstar sports stories over all the decades of the twentieth century, from Jim Jeffries to Wayne Gretzky, surely none is as improbable, nor as unbelievable, as the story of Fernando Valenzuela.¶ Let's see someone make up a story that can match this: we have a poor boy from Mexico, the youngest in a family of twelve. He grew up sleeping in the same bed with five brothers in a home with no running water. Until 1978, the home had no electricity. The boy wore hand-me-downs until he was eighteen. And in the dirt ball fields of his rural Sonoran village, Etchohuaquila, he learned in his early teens he could play baseball better than his older brothers. Or anyone else around.¶ You know the rest. Fernando Valenzuela winds up in Los Angeles, a hero to millions in two countries, and becomes a $2 million-a-year pitcher.

Everyone loves a success story. But if you'd dreamed this one up in the late 1970s and submitted it to a movie studio, they'd have laughed you off the lot.

The Los Angeles Dodgers' bird dog in Latin America, Mike Brito, had been following Valenzuela's development as a pitcher in Mexico's minor leagues. He'd turned pro at sixteen, and his first paycheck was for $250 for a three-month stint at Tepic. Next he pitched at Puebla, which briefly loaned its young left-hander to Guanajuato. Actually, Brito wasn't looking for Valenzuela; he'd come to look at a shortstop. He didn't like the shortstop. But he loved Guanajuato's sixteen-year-old left-handed relief pitcher. He asked a few questions, learned his name was Fernando Valenzuela, and that he had a 6–9 record but led the league in strikeouts.

Brito sent a glowing report back to the Dodgers' offices. Like a hound on the scent, Brito followed Valenzuela all summer. He continued to send enthusiastic reports to the Dodgers, and the club finally sent its chief scout, Charlie Metro, to take a look.

He was as impressed as Brito. Next came the Dodgers' general manager, Al Campanis. Serious negotiations were under way by July 1979. And just when the New York Yankees were stepping into the picture, the Dodgers purchased Valenzuela's contract from Puebla for $120,000, on July 6, 1979.

LEFT: Fernando Valenzuela was showing less than his best stuff in the third game of the 1981 World Series, but nevertheless subdued the Yankees.

RIGHT: Three Steves (Howe, Garvey, and Yeager) whoop it up after the visiting team's final putout in the '81 Series.

In the summer of 1979, Fernando Valenzuela came to the United States for the first time, to Lodi, California, to pitch in the Dodgers' Class A California League. He was the subject of great scrutiny by Dodger scouts. It was determined that while his mechanics were good, his fastball was barely major league level.

He needed another pitch. Bobby Castillo, a Dodger relief pitcher who'd mastered the screwball, was sent to the Arizona Instructional League for a sixty-day stint in the fall of 1979. The screwball is a reverse curve, and when thrown by a left-hander it breaks down and away from a right-handed hitter.

Valenzuela, in a relatively brief period, mastered the pitch. When he began his Texas League season at San Antonio in 1980, he became an instant sensation. He won his last seven games there, five of them shutouts.

The Dodgers called him up late in 1980, and at first he created more attention by his profile than his screwball. In his early Dodger years, Valenzuela was, to be polite, portly. And he had an odd delivery—he had a high leg kick, and at its peak his eyes would drift skyward, as if searching for an instant of concentration before releasing his pitch. And in his round, broad face, some saw a haunting resemblance to Babe Ruth. Odd, wasn't it, that Ruth had started out as a left-handed pitcher, too?

Valenzuela pitched well in his first few relief appearances, and won his first game in San Francisco, pitching two hitless innings in relief on a night when Pedro Guerrero hit a game-winning home run in the tenth inning. When the season ended, Valenzuela had pitched 17⅔ innings without allowing an earned run.

Valenzuela's star took off like a rocket in 1981. With his sweeping screwballs baffling one National League lineup after another, he won his first eight games—a major league record for a rookie. Five of them were shutouts. Suddenly, his face was everywhere, on newspaper sports pages and billboards. Seldom in the history of baseball had a player achieved star status so quickly.

And it all began on opening day.

The Dodgers began the season with a thin pitching staff due to injuries, and Valenzuela was called upon to start opening day. He beat Houston, 2–0, and "Fernandomania" was off and running.

The streak ended when Philadelphia beat Valenzuela, 4–0, in Los Angeles on May 18. After nine starts, he was 8–1 and had an earned run average of 0.91.

He finished the season at 13–7, with a league-leading eight shutouts. And he left behind a performance some considered, even years later, his greatest. The Dodgers were meeting the Montreal Expos in the National League Championship Series, and in the deciding game, on a cold, rainy night in Montreal, Valenzuela was the Dodger starter.

It was October 19, 1981, and Valenzuela was magnificent. All season long, he'd shown a natural talent. But on this night, he showed world-class poise, the ability to perform under pressure. On a night when he periodically seemed to lose his best stuff, he battled back from being behind on hitters in every inning. He gave up a run in the first inning, but retired eighteen of the next nineteen hitters. For the game, he allowed three hits. Valenzuela himself tied the game in the fifth with a single, and Rick Monday won it with a home run.

After that, the Dodgers beat the New York Yankees four games to two in the World Series. After that, Valenzuela went home to his family, to Etchohuaquila.

And this time, he got to sleep in a bed by himself.

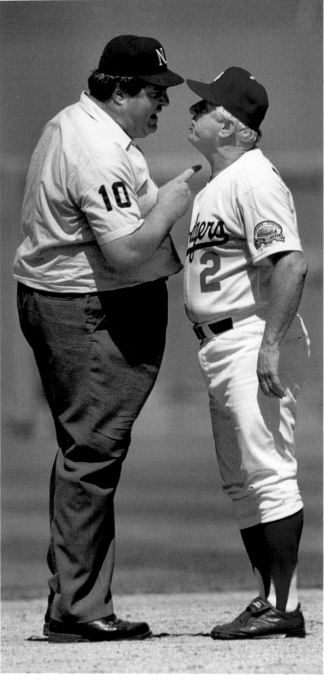

FAR LEFT, ABOVE: Sandy Koufax shows some of his old form as he keeps in shape pitching batting practice for his former team.

FAR LEFT: In 1983 Mr. October still had his eye on the fences, but the tobacco juice didn't get to first base.

LEFT: Dodger Stadium at twilight proved to be a happy place for many thousands of 1982 fans.

ABOVE: Dodger skipper Tom Lasorda shares some dieting tips with a friendly umpire.

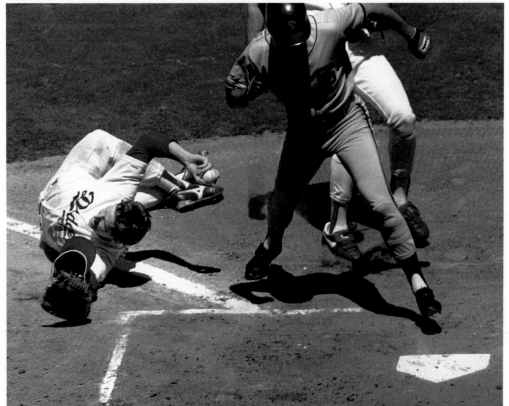

From time to time pitchers are asked to make putouts and two Dodgers here display their skills: Valenzuela made the force, though hanging onto the ball looks precarious; Hershiser missed the tag at the plate on Will Clark in a game that San Francisco went on to win 15–4.

The agony of defeat marks the posture of Patty Sheehan (above) as she misses a birdie try on the 18th at Mission Hills in the Nabisco Dinah Shore LPGA tournament in 1988. A year later, Julie Inkster jumped for joy as she sank a putt to win the event.

OVERLEAF: Breaking from the start at the Del Mar turf course, a line of thoroughbreds is a thing of beauty.

The two megastars of tennis in the 1980s, often seen in Southern California, were John McEnroe (shown during Davis Cup play at La Costa) and Martina Navratilova.

Opening of the trout season is a big sports event in any year; in 1986 it brought fishermen on foot and by boat in large numbers.

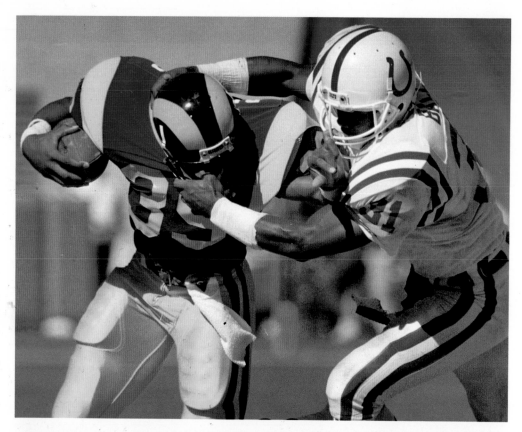

PRECEDING PAGES: Two Southern California rivals square off early in the 1986 season at the Coliseum, though even then owner Al Davis was looking to take the Raiders north again.

LEFT: Colts and Rams lock horns every time they meet, but this is going a little far.

BELOW: Will he or won't he; believe it or not, James Lofton made this reception, though for a time it looked like that was the last thing on his mind.

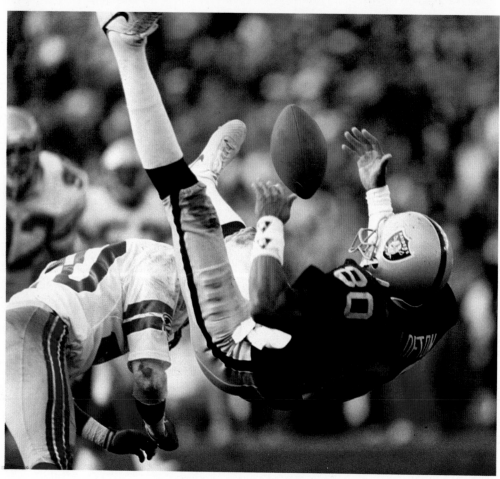

ABOVE: Marcus Allen had a Saint on his knees as he powered through for a big gain.

RIGHT: Troy Aikman is about to lose his shirt, but grips the ball tightly as he goes down for a loss.

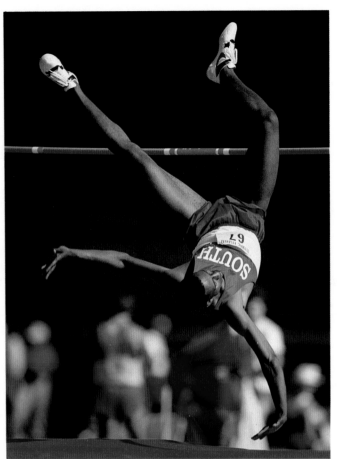

Pre-Olympic meets in 1984, as in any big year, brought competitors from all parts of the country to show their stuff. In the end, only a few went all the way to the Coliseum and fewer still went farther on their way to the victory stand.

ABOVE: In 1984 the Women's Marathon was a new event, and this competitor made some observers doubt that the women were up to it; but she finished the race, and once again the women had proved themselves equal to any task.

LEFT: At somewhat shorter distances, American women proved their strength, taking the 1,600 meter relay gold medal.

The opening parade at the 1984 summer games (right) went at a slow pace. Days later much faster walking was seen in the Coliseum as the 20 kilometer men's walk (below) was won by #632, Ernesto Canto of Mexico.

The Olympic motto "Farther, higher, stronger" is expressed in these three photos from 1984; of the 3,000 meter steeplechase, weightlifting, and pole vaulting. In that vault, Pierre Quinon of France took the gold.

Kareem Abdul-Jabbar played as hard as he ever had during his last season with the Lakers, and good-naturedly took a seat in the rocking chair his fellow players had provided for the old fellow. In the end, the normally well-controlled athlete couldn't hold back a few tears as a grateful audience said goodbye to one of basketball's greatest players.

In the 1976–77 school year, Earvin Johnson led his Everett High School team of Lansing, Michigan, to the state high school basketball championship. Two seasons later, as a sophomore, he guided Michigan State to the NCAA basketball championship. And one season after that, at age twenty, he led the Los Angeles Lakers to the NBA championship.

It's probably an unprecedented achievement, a prep-college–NBA championship run in so short a time span. But Earvin "Magic" Johnson is an unprecedented athlete. By the end of the 1980s, there was ample evidence that Johnson just might be the greatest basketball player who ever lived.

The NBA's two dominant players in the 1980s were two 6′9″ athletes who faced off in the 1979 NCAA title game, Johnson and Boston's Larry Bird, whose Indiana State team lost to Johnson's Michigan State team in 1979.

By decade's end, Johnson seemed to be alone, atop his game. During the 1988 Los Angeles–Detroit NBA championship series, the *Detroit News* polled thirty basketball writers, asking them to choose between Johnson and Bird. Johnson won, 28–2.

As a catalyst for a winning team, only Bill Russell of the 1950s and 1960s Boston Celtics could claim to have driven his team to more championships. The Johnson-powered Lakers were in the NBA finals seven times in the 1980s and won it five times.

Man of the decade for the Lakers
was without doubt Earvin (Magic)
Johnson.

America had never seen a basketball player quite like Magic Johnson. First, no one had ever seen a 6′9″ guard before, let alone one so gifted he could at times achieve complete control of a basketball game with passes that swept through defenses like cannon shots, and hands so quick that no opponents' passes were safe anywhere near him.

Oh, those passes. Only Oscar Robertson in NBA history was a more productive assist man. By 1989, of the nineteen 20-assist games in Laker history, Johnson had seventeen of them.

But most visible of all, no one had ever seen a basketball player who played the game with the intense joy of Magic Johnson. The NBA's great names of the past—George Mikan, Bill Russell, Wilt Chamberlain, Oscar Robertson, Jerry West, Julius Erving—inspired awe

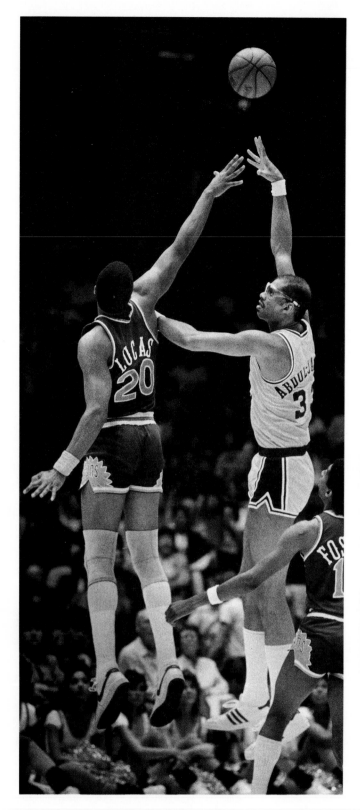

LEFT: The patented "Skyhook" was only one of the wicked ways that Kareem Abdul-Jabbar found to outwit the enemy.

Two former UCLA centers, who were briefly resident local opponents in the pro game, battle for dominance under the basket.

and respect with their talent. But Magic Johnson lights up an arena with his infectious enthusiasm as much as by his athleticism. He plays the game with a happiness that brings people to their feet laughing as well as shouting. It's as if he seems to want you to love the game as he does.

It wasn't cheers and laughs throughout the 1980s, though. In 1981, unhappy over Laker coach Paul Westhead's patterned offense, Johnson went to the team's owner, Jerry Buss, and complained. Buss fired Westhead. Headline:

"Buss Makes Westhead Disappear: It's Magic"

For a while, Johnson was booed at every arena in the league, by fans who apparently perceived Johnson as another overpaid, pampered, spoiled athlete. But it was all forgotten in time as Johnson began paving his road to the Hall of Fame with one brilliant season after another.

In 1984, Buss cut a deal with Johnson designed to insure the Lakers that his entire NBA career would be spent in Los Angeles. It was a landmark pro sports contract—$1 million a year for twenty-five years. But by the late 1980s, other NBA player contracts approached Johnson's, then passed it.

Finally, when Atlanta's center, Jon Koncak (who will go into the Hall of Fame only as a tourist) signed for $2.5 million per year, Johnson asked Buss to reshape the agreement. Result: the final $21 million of the original contract was condensed to seven years, meaning that Johnson will receive $3 million per season until 1993–94.

But to many, he could never top 1980, when as a boy he led a group of men to a championship. The 1980 Lakers came to the sixth game of the seven-game championship series with Philadelphia with a chance to score a knockout of the 76ers. One problem: they were without their all-star center, Kareem Abdul-Jabbar, watching at home with a sprained ankle.

The coach, Westhead, needed someone to fill in at center. Johnson, he decided. No way, most felt. It seemed then the Lakers' only hope was if Abdul-Jabbar could somehow recover for the seventh game. Johnson didn't see it that way. After Westhead announced Johnson would start at center, a straight-faced Johnson said: "I played some center in high school— no problem."

The date was May 16, 1980, and the 18,276 in the Philadelphia Spectrum should have known it was curtains when the players walked to center court for the opening tip: Johnson was the only player of the ten with a grin on his face. That's right. The NBA finals, and here's a twenty-year-old laughing at the pressure.

Magic Johnson scored forty-two points that night, grabbed fifteen rebounds, passed off for seven assists and was 14-for-14 from the free throw line. The Lakers led throughout, but the 76ers, with the home crowd roaring, closed to within 103–101 with five minutes to go.

Magic Time. Johnson, three seasons from his last high school season, scored eleven points down the stretch, and the Lakers outscored Philadelphia 20–6 over the final five minutes, to win by 123–107.

There was some irony attached to the fact that Johnson played Abdul-Jabbar's position in that championship game in his first NBA season. Just nine years earlier, the Abdul-Jabbar–led Milwaukee Bucks came to Detroit's Cobo Arena one afternoon and beat the

Detroit Pistons. Afterward, Abdul-Jabbar stood at his locker and talked to reporters. When the security guard wasn't looking, two young boys ran into the Bucks' locker room.

One of them carried a piece of paper and a pen. Finally, summoning his courage, the tall young boy thrust his paper and pen forward and asked for an autograph. Without a word, Abdul-Jabbar bent down and signed, and the young boy ran out, happy as a clam.

It was eleven-year-old Earvin Johnson.

On January 22, 1984, moments after a most improbable Super Bowl result, the Los Angeles Raiders' designated sorcerer, defensive back Lester Hayes, attributed the Raiders' smashing, 38–9 victory over the Washington Redskins to forces from another realm.

"The Silver and Black fears no mortal," he said. "We are Jedi. This was no surprise. Thursday night, a tremor from The Force stated to me that we were going to play a fantastic game."

Hayes, of course, was tuned into wavelengths no one else could pick up. But most saw Super Bowl XVIII as definable in more simple terms. It was a case of a good football team, the Redskins, experiencing the misfortune of catching a very good football team at its very best. In other words, a bunch of Raiders had career games and Los Angeles had its first NFL championship team since the Rams won the NFL title in 1951.

The magnitude of what the Raiders achieved in Tampa Stadium that Sunday afternoon was immediately apparent. The 12–4 Raiders took on a team that had won thirty-one of its previous thirty-four games, gave it its worst beating in five years, and won by the widest Super Bowl victory margin to date. It wasn't a game, it was an execution.

Much of the credit went to the Raiders' smooth, gliding running back out of USC, Marcus Allen, who ran for a Super Bowl–record 191 yards, including a spectacular 74-yard run on the last play of the third quarter. And some wanted to credit the old, steady hand at quarterback, thirteen-year veteran Jim Plunkett.

But in fact this was a game reduced to matchups, and in the most important matchups, the Raiders were clearly superior all afternoon long. Washington, with Joe Theismann at quarterback, had won the previous season's Super Bowl and rolled to a 14–2 record in the 1983 season by winning with home-run pass plays and its hammer.

The home-run players were long-pass receivers Charlie Brown and Art Monk. The hammer was one of the NFL's great fullbacks, John Riggins. The Raiders matched up the Redskins' deep receivers with Lester Hayes and Mike Haynes. With basic but brilliant man-to-man coverage, those two held Brown and Monk—who had caught a combined 125 passes for the season—to four receptions.

With the game then reduced to two nine-man teams, the rest of the Raiders' defense shut down the hammer. Focusing on Riggins, the Raiders' defense slam-dunked him, holding him to 64 yards on twenty-six carries and no touchdowns. In the regular season, Riggins had scored twenty-four touchdowns and gained 1,367 yards.

Toss in some big Raider plays, offensively and defensively, and the inevitable rout was under way. Los Angeles scored all the points it needed in the first half. The Raiders also were aided by a tremendous play by their punter, Ray Guy.

With a 14–0 lead, Guy was punting early in the second quarter. But long snapper Todd Christensen's snap was high, so high that Guy prevented a likely Washington recovery with a

LEFT: After missing a field goal at the end of regulation time, Raider kicker Chris Bahr lofted a 32-yarder in overtime to beat the Denver Broncos in November, 1985.

leaping, one-handed catch. And with twelve seconds left in the half, he punted to Washington's twelve-yard line, setting up another L.A. touchdown. To many, Guy's catch and punt was the play of the day, even greater than Allen's long run, which came in the third quarter.

Crowed Raiders managing general partner Al Davis afterward: "The play Guy made... Ray Guy is the greatest player of his position of all time."

On the last play of the first half, the Raiders' defense anticipated Theismann would not run out the clock but would pass. Little-known linebacker Jack Squirek was sent in and told to look for a pass. Theismann threw to his left, for Joe Washington, but Squirek intercepted in full stride at the five and loped into the end zone untouched.

The Redskins, starting the second half down by 21–3, scored their only touchdown on a 70-yard drive. But the Raiders countered with a scoring drive of their own, and it was 28–9

In the final seconds of the third quarter, Washington gambled on fourth-and-1 at the Los Angeles twenty-six, but linebacker Rod Martin tackled Riggins in his tracks.

Now came the backbreaker, one of the best-remembered plays of Super Bowl lore. On first-and-10, Allen broke the Redskins' hearts.

He took a Plunkett handoff and ran left, but found half the Redskin defense waiting for him. He veered 180 degrees, pivoted upfield, sped by some grounded Washington linemen, and outran everyone on the field to the end zone.

That made it 35–9, and a Chris Barr field goal made it the most one-sided Super Bowl ever, 38–9.

Those were the '83 Raiders, a happy, talented band of irreverent athletes who played it loose during the week but hard on Sunday. Five days before the Super Bowl, seven Raiders were fined $1,000 each for being late for a meeting, including Plunkett. Yawns all around.

They loved to needle their coach, Tom Flores, who at that point had spent nineteen of his twenty-four years in pro football with the Raiders.

Before the Super Bowl game, one of the Raiders, commenting on Flores's public speaking skills, said: "I wish you could hear his Monday-after-the-game speeches. He puts fifty guys to sleep."

It's hard to believe two one-hundred-pound women could create an international uproar by running into each other, but on August 10, 1984, at the Los Angeles Olympic Games, it happened.

When Zola Budd and Mary Decker Slaney came together on the fourth lap of the

San Francisco's Jeff Stover sent Jim Plunkett to the ground, and to the hospital with a shoulder separation, on September 22, 1985, as the Raiders fell to the 49ers 34–10.

Marcus Allen, former USC star and Heisman trophy winner, didn't rely on past glories to dominate the defense in this game against San Diego.

women's 3,000-meter final in the Los Angeles Memorial Coliseum, it was as if, at least for a few seconds, the world had stopped turning on its axis, waiting for Mary to get up.

In every Olympic Games, it seems, there's at least one incident that seems to overshadow even the Games themselves. In 1984, this was it. Decker, the twenty-six-year-old American and a solid favorite in the race, was the defending world champion in the event. Budd was the eighteen-year-old South African competing for England, competing in her first major international competition.

The two were at the head of a tightly bunched pack of runners as they passed the halfway point in the seven-and-a-half-lap race. Neither could have known that in a few seconds they were about to create the most sensational incident of the 1984 Olympics, or maybe of any other Olympics.

Budd, running in her trademark bare feet, had passed Decker and taken the lead on the Coliseum's tunnel-end turn. Then, about ten meters later, Decker seemed to be trying to take the lead back. She began to move by Budd near the track's curb.

Even after viewing video replay after video replay afterward, it was impossible to determine exactly what had happened in a split second, but it was clear that Decker's right foot had crossed Budd's left foot. Decker, suddenly unbalanced, threw out her arms, groping for something to hold onto. The only object she could grab was the paper number off Budd's back.

Decker tumbled onto the infield, and landed hard, face-first in the turf. Stunned, a crowd of over eighty thousand stared in disbelief at the frail figure on the grass, writhing and crying. The greatest women middle-distance runners in the world ran on, chasing a gold medal. But for millions watching the fallen runner, the race had become meaningless.

Binoculars were raised all over the Coliseum. Yes, that was Mary Decker, still down and out of the race. There would be no gold medal, but instead an ambulance ride to the hospital.

One of the lasting images of the incident is that of Decker's massive husband, discus thrower Richard Slaney, coming out of the stands, crossing the track, and picking up his tiny wife and carrying her away, her head buried in his neck.

Minutes later, as Decker was on her feet in the Coliseum tunnel, Budd approached her and seemed about to apologize.

"Don't bother," Decker said, waving her off. "I don't want to talk to you."

An hour after the race, after Decker had been examined at a hospital and been told she'd torn or strained a hip muscle, she talked to the media. "Zola Budd tried to cut in without being, basically, ahead," she said. "Her foot upset me. To avoid pushing her, I fell. Looking back on it, I should have pushed her."

Many observers agreed. Irish middle-distance runner Eamonn Coghlan said he thought Decker handled the crisis in too ladylike a fashion. "Look at the men's races, it happens all the time," he said. "Guys are shoving and bulling each other out of the way and nothing is ever said about it. It's part of running, protecting yourself."

At first, Budd was disqualified by race referee Andy Bakjian, but the British delegation protested and the disqualification was overturned by an eight-member appeals committee after thirty minutes of reviewing videotapes of the race.

Oh, the race. Budd, who'd been cut on her heel by Decker's shoe, was booed lustily by the crowd for the duration of the race. She faded to an eighth-place finish. The winner was Romanian Maricica Puica.

Barefooted Zola Budd skips past a tumbling Mary Decker as the American distance star's chance for an anticipated 1984 Olympic medal falls to earth.

Five years after the 1984 Olympics, Mary Decker Slaney and her husband, Richard, were the parents of a three-year-old daughter. At thirty-one, she was still an active runner.

Zola Budd, who as a young teenage runner in South Africa had Mary Decker's picture pinned to her bedroom wall, came into unhappy times in the years following the 1984 Olympics.

Hounded by London tabloids, she returned to South Africa and said she would never run again. She became estranged from her father, who was murdered in 1989. In his will, he directed that Zola and her sisters not be permitted to attend his funeral.

In a 1988 interview with the *Los Angeles Times*'s Julie Cart, Budd said that after Decker fell in the 1984 Olympic race, she slowed down. She explained, "I didn't think the people would have wanted to see me win a medal."

And when asked about what she enjoyed most about running, she said: "I think the best thing is, when I am running, I am alone."

In the closing weeks of the baseball season of 1988, pitcher Orel Hershiser put together a string of performances that might never be equaled. There were a record six consecutive shutouts and epic, winning performances in the National League playoffs and the World Series.

And the more the American sports public learned of Orel Hershiser, the more wide-

Grimacing in disappointment and frustration as much as pain, Mary Decker lies beside the track as the women's 3,000 meter final is won by Romania's Maricica Puica.

spread his appeal became. This guy, male sports followers realized, was one of them, all of them, any of them, each of them. He was Everyman.

He was the come-to-life fantasy figure for every American male who'd never made it on the football field, failed on the basketball court, or been cut from the baseball team.

In school, Orel Hershiser always looked more like the award-winning physics student than an athlete. He wasn't seven feet tall, he didn't weigh 300 pounds, and he couldn't bench press 400 pounds. He was instead a very ordinary-looking guy.

And so he became the walking, talking, American male dream—the nerd, magically transformed into the superathlete. You almost wondered if Dr. Frankenstein was somehow mixed up in this. Orel Hershiser: The Revenge of the Nerds.

He'd been cut from his high school baseball team, left off the traveling squad of his college team, and was the only player in his amateur hockey league who wore glasses. He eventually showed some promise as a college pitcher, and the Dodgers drafted him on the seventeenth round. Starting out, he was in over his head in the Texas League, where during one stretch he went three weeks without getting a single batter out.

On one weekend in El Paso, Hershiser gave up twenty-three runs in two outings. His ERA was 8.60.

Even when he reached the top of his profession, he looked like anything but a professional athlete, let alone like one of the great pitchers of his era.

He's skinny, seems bookish, has a pointed nose, a concave chest, wears uniform shirts that don't seem to fit, sings hymns for stress reduction, wears glasses off the field, and seems as if he'd be more at home managing a K-Mart.

The Dodgers started the 1980s by finding one unlikely looking superstar pitcher, Fernando Valenzuela, in Mexico. They finished the decade by finding another one at Bowling Green University in Ohio.

In the Dodgers' minor leagues, Hershiser bore the traits of virtually every other minor-league pitching prospect—promising stuff, but light-years away from putting it all together.

According to a Dodgers' minor league pitching instructor, it all came together for Hershiser in the winter of 1984. "In the Texas League and at Albuquerque [the Dodgers' triple-A team], Orel had good stuff," Dave Wallace said, "but because he didn't yet understand his own mechanics, he was inconsistent."

Hershiser, according to Wallace, has that one element that separates good pitchers from great ones: intelligence.

"Every pitcher who comes into pro ball has good stuff," Wallace said. "But none of them have the same stuff in every game. The great pitchers are the ones who can understand on a bad day, within three to five pitches, what the problem is and how to correct it. If it takes one or two innings, that's too long. They're out of there.

"Orel wasn't able to do that until the winter ball season of 1984, in the Dominican Republic. He'd spent the previous season at Albuquerque, pitched pretty well, and finished the season with the Dodgers. But that winter, in Santo Domingo, he brought everything together. For the first time, he fully understood his mechanics."

And what a difference one winter ball season made.

In 1983, Hershiser had pitched only eight major league innings, at the end of his Albuquerque season. In 1984, after he and Wallace had brought his game together in Santo Domingo, he pitched 182⅔ innings for the Dodgers and registered major league numbers. He was 11–8, with an earned run average of 2.66. And the Dodgers raised his salary from $47,000 to $212,000.

In 1985, he became a premier pitcher. He was 19–3 and had a 2.03 ERA. After that season, through arbitration, his salary zoomed to $1 million.

He had so-so 1986 and 1987 seasons, 14–14 and 16–16.

Then came 1988, and a Hall of Fame season—one that might never be equaled. Best remembered will be his six consecutive shutouts at the end of the season, a major league record fifty-nine consecutive scoreless innings.

Bear in mind, here's a guy who before 1988 had pitched eleven shutouts in 124 career starts. In just the two seasons preceding 1988, he'd thrown two in 70 starts. And now, six in a row, and each fashioned in the pressure of a pennant race. And yet, hard to believe, the best was yet to come.

The Dodgers beat the New York Mets to win the National League play-offs, then vanquished the favored Oakland As in the World Series in an astonishing five games. Hershiser was, in a word, brilliant. Throughout the play-offs and the World Series, it seemed

as if Hershiser had to crack, that the streak must surely end. It didn't. In a nation's spotlight, he was indomitable.

In six playoffs and World Series appearances, he was 3–0 with a save. His ERA was 1.05. In his last 101⅔ innings, including his record 59 consecutive scoreless innings (which snapped ex-Dodger Don Drysdale's major league record of 58, set in 1968), Hershiser allowed five runs. For the entire season, he was 26–8. Over his last thirteen starts, he was 9–0 and had a 0.59 ERA.

When it was over, Hershiser emerged with what at the time was the richest contract in baseball history: $7.9 million, through 1991. It works out to $81,387 per game.

No one, however, really expects him to ever equal 1988.

Footnote: Early in the 1990 season, Hershiser, after experiencing pain in his right shoulder, underwent surgery. The procedure was described as "major shoulder reconstruction," and many wondered if he would ever pitch effectively again.

Kirk Gibson, who won Game One of the World Series with a dramatic ninth-inning

*Times* photographer Thomas Kelsey catches the concentration and grit of Orel Hershiser as the Dodger ace shuts out Atlanta in September, 1988.

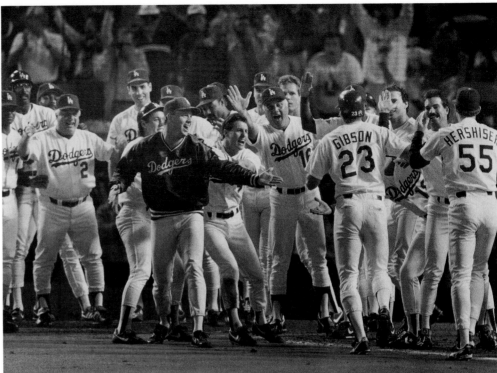

ABOVE: Kirk Gibson gets a free ride around the bases for his out-of-the-park blast in Game One of the 1988 Series. And lots of joy in Mudville greets Gibson after his game winning round tripper.

BELOW: Orel Hershiser delivers.

home run, summed up Hershiser's 1988 season best: "For as long as we live we may never see a pitcher accomplish what he's accomplished. We may never see a pitcher in a better groove for as long as he's been in this one."

Orel Hershiser's salary progression:

| Year | Salary | IP | W-L | SO | ERA |
|------|--------|------|------|-----|------|
| 1983 | $36,000 | 8 | 0-0 | 5 | 3.38 |
| 1984 | $47,000 | 182⅔ | 11-8 | 150 | 2.66 |
| 1985 | $212,000 | 239⅔ | 19-3 | 157 | 2.03 |
| 1986 | $1,000,000 | 231⅓ | 14-14 | 153 | 3.83 |
| 1987 | $800,000 | 264⅔ | 16-16 | 190 | 3.06 |
| 1988 | $1,100,000 | 267 | 23-8 | 178 | 2.03 |
| 1989 | $2,766,667 | 256⅔ | 15-15 | 178 | 2.31 |
| 1990 | $1,966,667 | | | | |
| 1991 | $3,166,667 | | | | |

For eighteen years, the Los Angeles Kings mucked along in the backwaters of major league hockey. There were a few play-off seasons, but for the most part, the team that Jack Kent Cooke put together in 1967 never appreciably raised the pulse rate of mainstream sports fans in Los Angeles.

Cooke himself once summed it up best: "When I started the Kings, I was told there were a quarter-million ex-Canadians in L.A. Now I know why they left Canada. They hate hockey."

Cooke, who after all once had brought Wilt Chamberlain to his Los Angeles Lakers basketball team, should have known that a superstar was needed to fix the Kings.

Cooke had long since departed for Washington when the Kings finally did something that excited Los Angeles. On August 9, 1988, the Kings' owner, Bruce McNall, brought hockey's Babe Ruth, Wayne Gretzky, from the Edmonton Oilers to Los Angeles.

It cost McNall two prized young players, three first-round draft choices, and $15 million, but someone had finally hauled hockey off the race-results pages in Los Angeles and put them on page one.

This was a very big deal. It rocked two countries. Seldom in professional sports history had a Hall of Fame–level athlete been sent from one team to another while still in his prime. In Canada, tears flowed.

"Wayne Gretzky is a national symbol, like the beaver," said National Democratic Party House leader Nelson Riis in Ottawa. "How can we allow the sale of our national symbols? It's quite simply unthinkable."

Said one Oilers ticket holder, Lana Polack: "He was born in Canada; he lived here—it's like he's defecting, going to the States."

In time, what was first seen as an act of national betrayal came to be seen as a sound business transaction for both the Kings and the Oilers. The Oilers' owner, Peter Pocklington, moved Gretzky at the best possible time for the Oilers. Gretzky, an eight-time National Hockey League MVP award winner, the holder of forty-one NHL scoring records, and the key contributor to Edmonton's four Stanley Cup championships in the previous five seasons, was only twenty-seven.

Further, Gretzky had four years remaining on his Oilers' contract. So Pocklington seized the opportunity presented, with Gretzky's value was at its peak, to rebuild his club. When the transaction was completed, here's what the Kings gave up to acquire Gretzky:

—Jimmy Carson, a twenty-year-old whose fifty-five goals in 1988 were an NHL record for a U.S.-born player. He was also only the second teenager to score fifty goals. The first was Gretzky.

—Martin Gelinas, eighteen, was an MVP from the Quebec Major Junior League and the No. 7 pick in the 1988 draft.

—The Kings' No. 1 draft picks in 1989, 1991, and 1993.

—$15 million.

Coming to the Kings with Gretzky were six-season veteran Mike Krushelnyski and Marty McSorley.

Years would have to pass to see who had achieved the better part of this deal, but after one season in Los Angeles, it was clear Gretzky had made hockey a major league sport in Los Angeles.

Indications came early. Within forty-eight hours of the announcement of the Gretzky deal, the Kings' ticket office reported one thousand calls inquiring about season ticket availability. When the season began, the Kings sold out (16,005) their opener for the first time ever and went on to post twenty-five sellouts in the 1988 season. Average attendance rose from 11,667 to 14,875.

And on the ice, Gretzky guided his new team to a smashingly improved season, 42–31–7, an improvement from eighteenth place to fourth. The Kings not only made the play-offs, they knocked off the defending champion Oilers before losing to Calgary, which went on to win the Stanley Cup.

Early in his second Kings season, Gretzky passed his boyhood idol, Gordie Howe, and

In 1972 a spindly Wayne Gretzky met his idol, then hockey's greatest star, Gordie Howe. By 1988 Gretzky was inspiring his Los Angeles teammates, plus hordes of Canadian and American youngsters with an amazing career.

became his sport's all-time leading scorer. And it happened, of all places, in Edmonton's Northlands Coliseum, before a capacity crowd of 17,503.

Gretzky did it dramatically, with style and grace, like a King. With fifty-three seconds left in regulation time, the record-breaker was a game-tying goal. Gretzky took a pass from Steve Duchesne and knocked the puck past Oilers goalie Bill Ranford. It was point number 1,851—he'd passed Howe and now stood alone, atop his sport.

Kings teammates and his former Oilers teammates skated onto the ice to congratulate him, and a ceremony ensued. His stick, jersey, and the puck were requisitioned and readied for shipment to the Hall of Fame.

But The King wasn't finished. On The Great One's greatest night, there was more. The game went to overtime. He won the game by darting from behind the Oilers' goal and scoring on a backhanded shot to give the Kings a 5–4 victory.

Skateboarding, California's newest contribution to athletics, has captured the fancy of teenagers all over America. As early as 1980, one of the sport's great stars, Christian Hosoi (right) of Venice, then 12 years old, was showing his form at the unique, tunnel-like skatepark at Marina del Rey; only a few years later, clothing and equipment makers, and television had caught onto the action (left).

Since 1979, experts have tried to identify why Gretzky could break a career scoring record in just eleven seasons when it had required twenty-six seasons for Gordie Howe.

"Wayne has an ability to see the entire playing surface in a way other players can't," says longtime Kings announcer Bob Miller.

"There's another theory that's been applied to Wayne, the theory that was applied to Elgin Baylor. Remember how it seemed Baylor could hang in the air with the basketball a split second longer than the defender? Wayne does that with the puck—he hangs onto it a split second longer than the defender does.

"As a skater, Wayne does one thing better than anyone and that's stop on a dime and change direction—almost like O. J. Simpson."

It is a measure of Gretzky the man that during the ceremony celebrating his record score, his former Edmonton teammates presented him with a diamond bracelet weighing 1,851 carats, representing the new NHL career points record.

The inscription on the bracelet: "A great man is made up of qualities that meet or make great occasions. Presented in friendship by the Edmonton Oilers Hockey Club, 1989–90."

FAR LEFT: Clad in stars and stripes, bouncy Mary Lou Retton scores a perfect 10 in the vault to take a gold medal at the 1984 Los Angeles summer games.

LEFT: Television City's Dinah Shore put some oomph in LPGA golf with the long-lasting Nabisco event that bears her name. And in 1987 at Mission Hills Country Club, Pat Bradley added some oomph herself as she sank a birdie putt on the difficult 18th hole, winning the tourney the next day.

LEFT BELOW: Women's sports took off in the 1980s, beginning to earn equal attention at many levels.

RIGHT: Rising star Zina Garrison brought a new athleticism to women's tennis, as she demonstrates here competing in a Virginia Slims event at Manhattan Beach in 1986.

ABOVE LEFT: Steve Timmons of the United States men's volleyball team gives the fist of victory as the U.S. defeated Argentina at Long Beach in the 1984 Olympics. The U.S. went on to gold medal in those summer games.

ABOVE RIGHT: Through the 1980s soccer took hold in the U.S., though no professional league could be sustained. These players from Esperanza High School in Orange County, grittily defending a direct kick by Coachella High in a 1989 game, give hope that youth soccer will build a wider audience for the most popular international sport.

Dennis Connor made his first America's Cup defense in San Diego waters, losing to Australia. Taking the Cup back from the Aussies in Fremantle, Connor was later forced to defend it at home against a New Zealand challenger, winning the race in a controversial catamaran (below left), then losing it and winning it again in court in 1990.

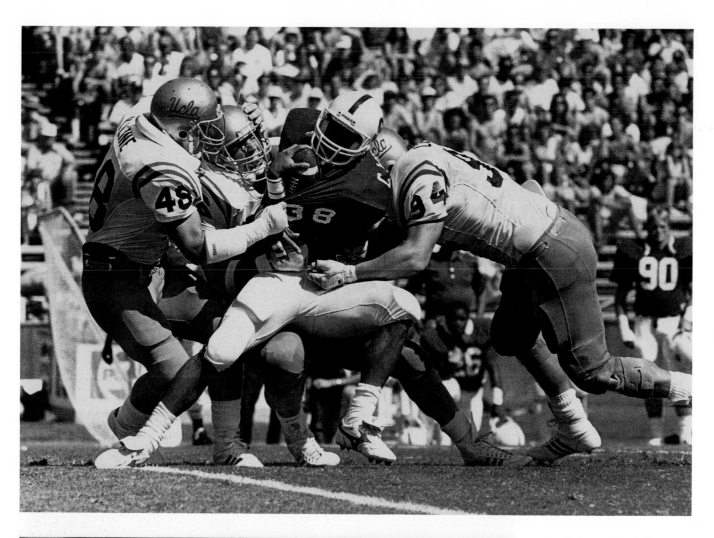

ABOVE: In the ongoing rivalry between the North and South of California, UCLA Bruins made their weight felt as Doug Kline (48), Mike Lodish (94), and a teammate halt Stanford's Charlie Young during a 1987 49–0 victory.

LEFT: L.A.'s Manual Arts High School coach John Engelman was understandably perturbed when he found one of his players on the bench when he was supposed to be on the field. Despite this lapse, Manual teams won the 3A city championship two years in 1983 and '84.

Despite the impressive number of stickers on his helmet, one of Bo Schembechler's Michigan players seems to require additional instruction as his team meets USC in the Rose Bowl.

# EPILOGUE

**I**t's almost over, this century of sports. In less than a decade, after we put the 1990s to bed, we'll start another one.

I thought about this one weekday afternoon at the Rose Bowl, during the time I was writing the 1920s chapter of this book. I discovered that Tunnel B at the Rose Bowl is always open during the week, for out-of-town visitors who've never seen the old, famous stadium.

I walked in, alone. I'd never been alone before in a 103,000-seat stadium. The silence seemed suffocating, until I started listening for distant echoes.

I remembered something from an old college science book. It had to do with physics, that a sound, arguably, never dies but instead continues into infinity, ever-diminishing, but never dying.

So in the eerie quiet of the Rose Bowl, I wondered if the commotion, the terrible excitement, and the shouts of the crowd during Roy Riegels's incredible wrong-way run that New Year's Day in 1929 were still bouncing around in the old stadium, far beyond human hearing.

And that made me wonder what Southern California followers of sports will think, a century from now, of our century. The Rose Bowl, for example. Will it still be here? Will young men still play football? Or will chariot racing make a twenty-first century comeback? And what of baseball, basketball, horse racing, track and field, and everything else we've watched in our time?

Moreover, will twenty-first century Southern Californians actually *go* to places like the Rose Bowl, the Coliseum, Santa Anita, or Dodger Stadium? Or will traffic be so bad by then that they'll be a society of high-tech couch potatoes—at home, watching their century go by on pay-per-view, high definition television?

In the solitude of the Rose Bowl that afternoon, I decided I'd take the twentieth century.

Earl Gustkey
April 8, 1990